My Dearest Annie

John McCullen

 www.trafford.com

North America & international
toll-free: 1 888 232 4444 (USA & Canada)
fax: 812 355 4082

Cover design by Susan Rooney

By the same Author:

The Call of St. Mary's (1984)

The Brass Thimble (1996)

Jingles of the Harness (1999)

Acknowledgements

I wish to express my gratitude to my immediate and extended family, who conserved the material which I used, stripped their walls to provide photographs, racked their brains for memories of times past and were generous with their welcome.

My particular gratitude for advice and resources is due to Arthur McKevett, Noel Ross, Diana McCarthy-Lynch, The O'Malleys of Millextown, John McGovern, Jim Garry, Ann Mitchell, Rita Towell, Philip King, Mary Fuller, Deirdre Russell, Pat Hanratty and The Old Drogheda Society, Trafford Publishing, in the person of Tom Reilly, F.B.D. Insurances, Fr. Michael Murtagh, Gerry Cullen, Seán Corcoran and Anne Cassin.

In creating the book, an enormous amount of work on layout and design was done by Dermot McCullen and Susan Rooney and I deeply appreciate the constant back-up from Peter, Ruth, Jason, Grace, Lucy and Colm. Enthusiastic moral support, practical assistance and innumerable searches were provided by my wife, Ann, whom I thank unreservedly.

My hope is that the emergence of Annie and her writing companions from the shadows of the past will enthuse, fascinate and inspire the reader.

John McCullen
November 2003

To Doctor Oliver McCullen,
an influential Godfather,
on the occasion of his 80th birthday.

She makes her life one grand beatitude

Of Love and Peace, and with contented eyes

She sees not in the whole world mean or rude,

And her small lot she trebly multiplies.

Still to be happy is her sole desire,

She sings sweet songs about a great emprise,

And sees a garden blowing in the fire.

- from *The Gardener* by Francis Ledwidge

Chapter One
The Eldest Girl

     Two ingredients for a good story have always been a battle and a mill by the river. Any heroine had both in her background. Annie Moore lived from 1854-1915 and was the eldest girl of nine children born to Richard Moore and Mary Hoey. Richard was from a family who had reputedly come from Laois to engage in the Battle of the Boyne in 1690, and settled locally, while the Hoeys came from Whiteriver, Co. Louth, then a peaceful trout-fishing river with a thriving water mill, now the scene of a dump construction controversy. Moores owned a public house cum general store at Duleek Gate, Drogheda, which Richard had purchased in the early 1840s. His brother John had a grocery shop on the opposite side and was Mayor of Drogheda in 1861. While the Moores may have been engaged in the Battle in 1690, they did not make a direct journey from Laois, because Richard's great-great-grandfather, Patrick, was settled at Ballantry, Barony of Dunboyne, during his lifetime (1606-1701) and would have been a bit old to be a Jacobite soldier. He is buried in Kilbride old Churchyard, on the borders of Meath and Dublin.

Richard Moore (1820-1878), father of Annie

Mary Hoey Moore, Annie's mother

Annie married Patrick McCullen on Wednesday, February 2nd, 1881, in St. Mary's Church in Drogheda and they had eight children, seven sons and one daughter. Their honeymoon was spent at Knock and the couple lived at Beamore, in a two-storey farmhouse which they extended about 1890.

When Annie died on Sunday, June 20th, in 1915, she was in her 61st year but none of her own children had yet married. In the years following she became grandmother of twenty-one grandchildren, the first of whom Nancy (Ball) was born in 1917 to Joe and his wife, Sissy Gillic.

None of those grandchildren knew their grandmother, except through the eyes, and memories of her husband, family and contemporaries. The recently discovered letters, along with existing ones, safeguarded by her daughter Mary, enable us to build a picture of Annie which demonstrates her abilities, charm, spirituality and strength of character.

A school report is often a useful means of gaining clues to a character…

Sienna Convent,

DROGHEDA.

Report of Pupil's Progress

from _September_ to _Christmas_ Examinations

Miss _Moore_ 1868

	Class	Good	Bad		Class	Good	Bad
Health,				Sacred History,	2ᵈ	20	
Conduct,		48	2	General ditto,	"	23	1
Christian Doctrine,	2ᵈ	20	2	Natural ditto,			
Politeness,		50		Elements of Natural			
Order,		39	11	Philosophy,			
Reading,	"	27	1	French,	4ᵗʰ	30	
Spelling and				Italian,			
Dictation,	"	26		German,			
Writing,	3ᵈ	14		Music (Instrumental,)	"	11	3
Arithmetic,	1ˢᵗ	16		Singing,			
English Grammar,	2ᵈ	22		Drawing,			
Geography,	"	16	2	Painting,			
Use of the Globes,				Needle Work,	3ᵈ	20	
Composition,	"	17					

Sʳ M. Joseph

When the report was written in 1868, Annie was aged 14 and had already seen the deaths of Andrew, aged 4 and Bedelia, 3 months, and her older brother had died at 5 months of age, eight months before Annie was born. There had also been seven births in her 14 years and a shop, general store and public house to run. The progress measured by Sr. Joseph places her second in the class in most subjects, but first in Arithmetic, awards maximum marks for "Politeness" and yet she manages to get 11 bad marks for "Order". This suggests a bright, mannerly girl who is more than a bit giddy!

Being the eldest surviving child in the family must have placed great expectations on Annie as an assistant to her mother, a minder to her brothers and sisters, and as a worker in the shop. While the emotional pressure of all the deaths and pregnancies may appear very great in 2003 terms, it was not unusual in post-famine Ireland and it is important to remember that Richard himself was a child of a father, John, who married three times had three families, totalling fourteen children, at least two of whom were called John.

The extract below, from the Moore Family Bible, tabulates Annie's family of origin.

Richard & Mary married 3/2/1853		
John b.23/11/53		d.6/4/54
Annie b.1/12/54		
Richard 13/9/56	-	12/85
John A. 27/12/57	-	June 1876
Andrew 16/6/59	-	13/6/63
Mary Jane 23/1/61	-	m. P. Macken 4/03
Teresa 23/9/62	-	26/1/1946
Mary 18/3/66	-	entered convent 3/3/96
Bedelia 3/7/67	-	25/8/67
Richard d. 3/7/78		
Mary d. 9/2/90		

View of Moore's Pub (as Flynn's 1990)

(the residence is at the right-hand side)

In a letter dated June 4th, 1867, Annie writes to her Mamma —

We are very glad Saint Aloysius' day is coming. I hope as usual you will make a pie for me, we expect to have our feast very grand this year…I must exert myself to sell a great many tickets for the Christian Brothers' Bazaar…

On the back of the letter is a P.S. written by Sr. Aloysius —

I would be very glad to have Nanny made to practise at least one hour and a half every day. She is not improving as much in her music as she otherwise would. She is better for the last few days.

DEATH OF CAPTAIN R. MOORE.

It is with feelings of deep and sincere regret, which, we are sure, will be shared in by many, that we record the death of Captain Richard Moore, the only son of Mrs. R. Moore, Duleek-street. The deceased had but a short time ago got his certificate as captain, and was on his voyage from Philadelphia to London, when on the 5th ult, his vessel (Colchester) was running in a fierce gale of wind and shipped a heavy sea aft, which washed the two men at the wheel overboard and filled the cabin with water. At the time Captain Moore was in the fore part of the poop and was swept also overboard, and nothing could be done to save him. His only brother met with the same fate a few years ago.

Captain Moore was of a quiet and retiring disposition, and greatly liked by all who knew him. He was an affectionate and dutiful son, a fond brother and a sincere and warm hearted friend. He was only in the 29th year of his age when the angry sea engulphed him. To his bereaved widowed mother and sorrowing sisters we offer our sincere sympathy, in this sad hour of their affliction. R.I.P.

Chapter Two
The Donor Letters (1867-1878)

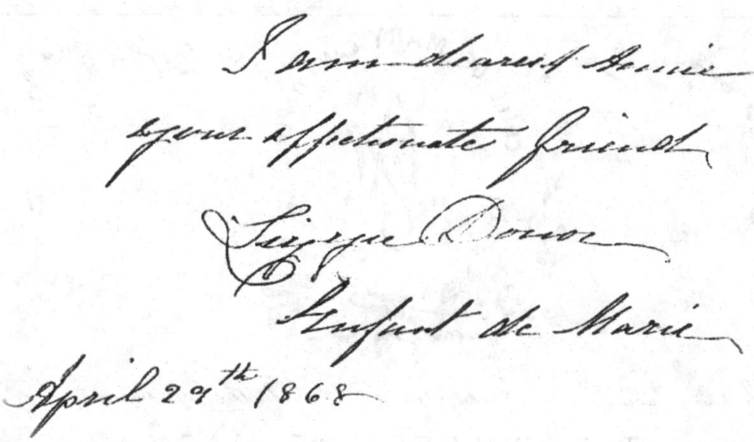

[handwritten signature]

These are written by Lizzie Donor, whose father was the Borough Engineer responsible for the 3-acre park laid out in 1850 under the Boyne Viaduct, Drogheda, on the North side of the river, and called "Donor's Green". The letters are sent from Greenhills in Drogheda, a furnished apartment at Charles St., Limerick, No. 2, Millview Tce., The Mall, Limerick and Mallow, Co. Cork. Mr. Donor features in a report of a meeting of the Boyne Commissioners, written in the Drogheda Argus of April 25th, 1863. A debate had arisen about the concerns of the Inspector of Fisheries, Mr. Lanney. Mr. Donor said that he takes a walk along the place alluded to every morning, and that instead of the great destruction represented, not a dozen of the small fish were destroyed. It would cost the Board £50 to do what Mr. Lanney asked them to agree to.

Somewhat frustrated at the attitude of a Mr. P. Boylan, Mr. Donor reacted angrily – "If the protection of a few stray fish are of more importance to you than the navigation of the river, I have nothing to say!"

It seems that Mr. F.J. Donor died in 1867 and his wife and five daughters, Johanna, Kate, Mary Anne, Bridget and Lizzie then moved to Limerick, much to the grief of Lizzie, who pined for Drogheda and her school friends, acted as carer to her ailing Mamma, was horrified when her sister Johanna left home to become a nun in Drogheda with the Sisters of Charity and was angry with her brother who had become a priest.

Her first letter at the age of 12-13 years is light and gentle, to a fellow child of Mary.

Greenhills
December 31st, 1867

Dear Annie,

I received your kind note and I assure you I am very grateful for your nice little souvenir of Christmas. I hope you enjoyed vacation. I suppose you spent most of your time reading the Irish History. I am sure it is very interesting.

I have read Valerie's Mamma and all of us like it very much. Johanna says if you say <u>three</u> <u>Hail Marys</u> for her every day she will lend you Percy Grange as long as you continue to say them even if it were for a year. I am not as fond of prayers Annie nor I don't think you are either. I hope your dear Papa is quite recovered and that Mamma, brothers and sisters are all quite well. Johanna and Kate send you their best love and accept the same from me. Adieu dearest Annie and believe me your ever fond sister in Mary.

L.Donor

New Year's Eve. P.S. Don't forget to come to the Convent tomorrow and bring your Festival ribbon and medal. L.D

Charles Street,
Limerick.
June 24th, 1868.

My dearest Annie,

It is with feelings of deep gratitude that I write to you first of all to thank you for your nice little collar and secondly for your kindness in writing to me a second letter before I had the politeness to answer your first. I hope your Mamma is very well after her long journey and also that your Papa is nearly quite recovered. When do you expect himself and Richie home? Did Miss Farrell's reception take place as yet? I suppose you were invited. Isn't Fr. Dardis's month's mind to take place today? Father Jackman is gone there so we will have a great deal of news from Drogheda. I think Father Keating went also but I am not sure. The Nuns I suppose have not given vacation yet. I hope it is the last vacation they will have to give you. Mamma got a letter from Father Murphy lately he said that James Connolly was married to Miss Saul I suppose it is the whole theme through Drogheda. Mamma and Johanna and all of us send our kindest love to your Mamma, Jonny, and all your sisters not forgetting yourself dearest Annie and believe me to be

Your ever loving friend Lizzie Enfant de Marie.

Please tell Alicia Farrell to write soon and do the same yourself.

The 1867-1869 letters are edged with black, denoting two years of mourning for Mr. Donor, and there are 49 letters in total.

Charles St.,
Limerick.
July 1868.

…I am delighted to hear that you got your ears pierced. I hope they are not very sore with you. I intend to get mine pierced again when the weather gets colder…I am sure your dress is very nice. Do not forget to send a bit of it when writing.

Charles Street,
Limerick
September 15th, 1868.

My dearest Annie

I hope you will excuse me for not writing answering your very kind letter with your lovely photograph. I have to congratulate you on looking so nice and in having it so well taken.

I would have written sooner but as I suppose you have heard by this my dear sister Johanna is gone to Drogheda to be a Nun. She took a great liking to the Sisters of Charity when they used to visit poor Papa but she kept it to herself and it is only very lately she told Mamma or indeed dearest Annie I would have told you about it. Mamma thought it is a Sister of Mercy she would be and that she would remain in Limerick near us but she would not stop here or let Mamma speak about being a Nun here at all. A cousin of ours went to be a Sister of Mercy here on Saturday last, she is a niece of Fr. McMahon. He came here with her and they breakfasted and then went off to the Convent. He took Bridget home with him for some time. I am sure they will have great fun as they have a garden and orchard. He also has two young curates. Mamma desires me to tell your Mamma that Mr. Crimmin is dying and no hope of him he has a son a doctor in Dublin

Undated

Charles St.

I like the city pretty well, it is very large, and I think much warmer than Drogheda. The churches here are beautiful, especially the Redemptorist…

We were delighted to see your dear Papa and Uncle John who were so kind to come to see us. They could not stop long as it was late when they arrived but short as they stayed, they didn't forget to give the youngsters plenty of money. Mamma did not know it to thank them, until they were gone. Mamma was so overjoyed to see him look so well, after he being ill…

The Nuns have a grand boarding school — it is called Laurel Hill Convent. We were asking Papa to send you a boarder. I wish he did, you would be so near us we could often go to see you!

No. 2, Millview Tce., Mall,

Limerick. July 27th, 1869.

Our brother Jonny took a notion, and went off to New York, Mamma and us all felt so lonesome…I am getting to like the city better every day. Our home is nicer than the one we lived in before. There is a little garden in front, and the water opposite the door.

August 19th, 1869.

Delighted to hear that Papa and Mamma had gone to Lisdoonvarna…Captain Kelly of "The Jane" and his son were here last week, and came to see us…We received a letter from Johanna, very well and happy and asking us all to become Sisters of Charity. What an idea! Fr. O'Byrne called to see us today…

Millview Tce.

Wednesday (no date)

We heard from Mr. Murtagh who is here in a Doctor's shop that scarletina was prevalent in Drogheda. I trust it has not visited your street…

January 1ˢᵗ, 1870.

We are in second mourning now and black dresses are so fashionable that I don't want to leave it yet…(all the letters since 1867 have been with black edging, presumably in mourning for her "Papa".)

May 26ᵗʰ, 1870.

My same old scribble, but your writing is really beautiful!

August 21ˢᵗ, 1870.

It is kind of you to make apologies to me who is negligent…I could never for a moment believe it was through ill nature you did not write. I know your heart is too good and too noble to allow such a feeling. We were very sorry to hear of the accident that happened poor Richie. I am sure your Mamma must have got a great fright and himself the poor fellow was so much hurt, I trust in goodness he'll soon be quite well again…

July 27ᵗʰ, 1871.

…I hope none of your friends got the smallpox as I believe it was very prevalent in Drogheda – 184 – we saw by the paper, the Argus. There were only very few cases of it in Limerick. This is a very healthy place.

Wednesday (undated)

I write to enquire how Jonny is going on. I trust as well as ever now. I suppose he suffered a great deal with having it amputated. Have you heard lately from Richie?

March 13ᵗʰ, 1872

You must be quite a full-grown young lady, I suppose. You will be glad to hear that Michael has come home from Rome for ordination.

June 9ᵗʰ, 1872

I am sorry to hear that your Mamma was not too strong. Mamma has not been well for three weeks…read of poor Alice Farrell's death in the Argus…had not the least idea that she was soon to be no more…

Christmas Eve '72

Your letter would induce anyone to correspond, but you are dealing with a rather negligent friend in poor Lizzie! Have you many brothers and sisters now? Very like your Mamma feels she has a treasure in her eldest daughter, I suppose quite a young lady!

October 11ᵗʰ, 1873

…breaking this silence that has existed between us for so long…negligence on my part…my affection for you is deeper than ever…I often think of poor Sissy's innocence at school. At the rate things are going now, I wouldn't be surprised if I heard of your marriage or reception, the latter I suppose you prefer, if you be faithful to the sayings of old times. As for me, I might be an old maid but still it would be the last resource — you may say such nonsense.

November 1ˢᵗ, 1873.

Your forgiving disposition and soft heart will allow me to excuse myself the delay in writing to thank you for your carte, with the same nice innocent look! I did not get mine taken, because I am not very tall and handsome.

December 23ʳᵈ, 1873.

Now what about yourself? I am inclined to envy you — you are such a pet…

Millview Tce.,
March 17ᵗʰ, 1874.

My dear Annie,

Your thumb must have been very painful — it's such a dangerous part, I suppose it weakened you very much, still you may be very thankful to escape so well. I trust you are quite over it now. M. Hogan is at the Franciscans — he is very nice, but still I'd expect him to be more polished. Johanna was professed on the 2ⁿᵈ Feb. last. We were sent some of the cake and a number of pictures. I had a note from Rev. Mother- she said Johanna was well happy and only had to become a <u>Great</u> <u>Saint.</u> Did you ever hear such sayings as those Nuns have?

It was sad to hear of Miss Greene's death. I believe she was the youngest. I almost envy young people when I hear of their deaths and they in the nice position she was in to prepare for death. I mean it's a Perpetual Adoration Convent…why are you not provided for after Shrove? I would not have been so much surprised if I heard you were gone to a Convent or married either of course you want to be an <u>old maid</u>. As for meself I am nearly on the shelf. I suppose you know the Sub Inspector of Duleek – his wife is a Limerick lady, a Miss McMahon. The other home we lived in her father owned it – it's said she got two thousand pounds fortune.

June 29th, 1874

I would approve very much of your Aunt's prudence in having her girls sent as Boarders to Dalkey. They will have such an opportunity of learning things they would not be taught at a day school. For my part I can't cease to regret how much I misspent my time at school…

December 1st, 1874

I visited Dublin lately, and liked it very well. It is time for me to stir myself – they had me on the childish line long enough…I fear I will never enjoy such happiness as Johanna does…

December 25th, 1874

I must console with you dearest Annie about your brothers. It must have been a great shock to you all especially Mamma when the accident happened Jonny – it was fortunate he escaped even so well, but still the idea of losing his finger is awful. I trust he is getting on well. I really am surprised to hear about poor Richie and I think it a pity he did not make a better choice…it is such an uncertain and hard life, for such a nice boy; I suppose your Mamma can console herself that when he had a taste for the sea, it wasn't out of her way to allow him go.

My brother Jonny had a taste for the sea but was at Boarding school, and a fee paid for him here…he might as well have gone to sea, as he has not written to us this length of time…some one saw him in America.

Undated.

A head of sense such as yours…you'll go with your parents' wishes! No doubt you have a few admirers (I wouldn't like many). Are they Drogheda gents? Have you seen Richie's likeness? I'd like to see it. I'm ugly enough not to have a carte taken…

May 6th, 1875.

I was making lilies for the Franciscan Church – they were very tedious, but looked beautiful, when finished. Have you learned flowers at the Sienna Convent? Now even the passion flower has become easy to me.

I am thinking of going into some occupation, as I am tired of my life after long years so idly spent. Don't mention anything about it. Mamma and my brother are not too pleased at idea. Would you advise me to do it? How have you learned to write such a hand? Was it at Sienna?

Mallow.

September 10th, 1875.

I decided on going to business and gave up corresponding. This is a pretty town…I am apprenticed to Mr. Welsley. He and his wife are the only family, so I am not annoyed with youngsters. Three more apprentices, and myself, learning millinery, sales and the machine…If I were at home I'd consider better again.

How delighted Teresa Levins' father was to have her be a nun…surprised that Josephine is a widow now…her husband and mother in law used to look very strange, going down the green by themselves…we used call them Germans…I only pity young girls when they are married. Would you advise me to it? How is Katie McCann? <u>How have you learned to write such a hand? Was it at Sienna?</u> I've idled my time greatly at school so now I'm repaid with my writing! You must say to me what you intend doing with yourself. At all events never go to the Convent without letting me know saying "goodbye". If you intend being married be even more particular in doing so, then I'll be able to tell you the edifying manner in which they act in Limerick both in the way of getting good religious husbands and themselves preparing as if in fact they were going to be Nuns. Now amn't I the great adviser…an old maid…all the grand ladies unprovided for here.

I fancy all their enjoyment is at an end. Is it not a fact? At all events, I think so, no matter how rich they are. Did you go to M. Reilly's yet?

Sometimes I feel so lonely, I almost cry and indeed cries when writing. I be anxious for Drogheda news…does Sr. Evangelist look young now? Please send me a long letter.

Mallow,

December 5th, 1875.

    I suffer from chilblains and my hands are swelled. Old business dames are always so particular and I think no one can do anything right but themselves; at all events, Mrs. Wesley has a touch of that in her. I often regret how little I appreciated my mother – she being so soft and easily pleased…

    You are well worth spending money on, if you are in accordance with your carte, really it was very much praised.

Mallow,

December 31st, 1875.

Ever dearest A.,

    Not forgotten <u>poor me</u>…Katie didn't send me some cards…hurry of business before Xmas enjoying the pleasure of Richie's company – can say with more certainty than ever "there's no place like home" not my own mistress! Even more dainties than at home but what's that in comparison…Michael was there so that caused me more to feel unable to enjoy his company. How many brothers and sisters have you now – I haven't an idea. <u>Do you keep up the old custom of dining at your Uncle's for Christmas Day?</u> I saw Alice Healy's death on the Freeman – was it consumption she had?

    I'm just pitied by Michael especially as nothing would do me but go away to business. You asked about my lovers but didn't you know that my apprenticeship put things like that out of the question even that I were inclined for such stuff and besides to tell the truth I am not over anxious for the married life, for very often it brings so much troubles with it. What an old maid you'll say for after all when asked it's time enough to refuse. Now are you going on a very sensible line in these matters?

Mallow,

February 22nd, 1876.

    Is J. Healy's wife a Protestant still? Has she many children do you know? I thought her very pretty long ago. How is Jonny – you never speak of him. I'm as lonely as can be this past fortnight – Katie is gone to Boarding school in England – Monmouth St. Joseph's. She was more like an elder sister than a younger one…I can't refrain from crying…fancy she would not get her carte taken. Without boasting, she was the most passable of our family…dark and tall.

Undated.

I would give a good deal were I like you. I have changed greatly since I came to Mallow. I got less religious and less taste for praying and that…I require prayers…Are you going to the sea at all this Summer? You can't be spared, I suspect.

March 4th, 1876.

Thank you for the cartes of Richie and Jonny – I'd never know Jonny. He is so grand and as for Richie, he changed wonderfully, since I saw him, he is so manly looking. His carte was <u>very</u>, <u>very</u>, much admired. I am as discontented as could be – Mrs. W. is as particular, then as peevish, being delicate; at all events, I wish I'd got a nicer place to serve my time. When one has not got a vocation, I think knowing business is very essential, especially when I haven't got a very large fortune…

I don't wonder about you not visiting Sienna, they were very distant Nuns, not like the Sisters of Charity. I couldn't bear Ms. Mary Catherine, is she anything more gentle? Are you as fond of the fashions as ever? Do you often go to Dublin?

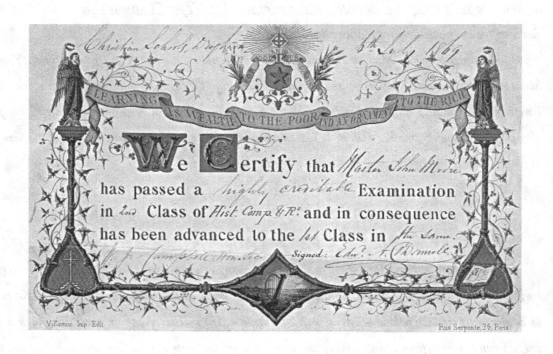

Richie Moore (1856-1885)

March 21ˢᵗ, 1876.

You have a good kind heart…I never like that outside friendship but to have real sincerity with anyone I make a friend of is my object, and then it's my pleasure to confide in, and correspond with. I am glad you have been so well pleased with the Redemptorists. The Limerick people are quite good, through their guidance, and be models of piety to strangers…

Mallow May 7ᵗʰ, 1876.

You are so well off! What is his name and how old is "he"?…I am surprised at Maggie McCann's purpose to be a nun. Was it the Mercy Nuns got the convent for her? Had she a fortune do you know?…I'll not be surprised in the least if I learn someday you've entered some convent! Mrs. Daly's first cousin, Delia Cronin went to school with me, but when she entered Laurel Hill, she never said one word of goodbye to me….perhaps she was forbidden?

Mallow,
Sunday (undated).

I feel very much for your Mama's anxiety about poor Jonny. But now Annie, there is no use in fretting, but have more confidence in the Blessed Virgin. I believe she will grant your desires through Mary Immaculate.

I got my carte taken – as ugly can be, but sent it to Katie, and she kept it. I will get one soon for you. Let me know news of Jonny. Burn this when read…

March 18ᵗʰ, 1877.

I almost vowed I would not write any letters for the next twelve months…all responses were so very short, and I include yours in the numbers, too, Miss Annie! I have not written to Johanna or Katie for two months…she is Sr. M. Winifrede now, but I am indifferent, she is lost to me forever…

Perhaps your cousins are waiting for you to give them example, and <u>enter</u>. It's a real wonder to me why so many girls enter convents.

Mallow,
December 23ʳᵈ, 1877.

I feel more than could be imagined…not a word from you for the last year almost. After Xmas I expect a long letter…I will send one in return.

Undated.

…Thanks for the slipper pattern work…you decide…you are so experienced about Berlin wool work…

Mallow,

Sunday (undated).

Thanks for letter received on Wednesday. Mallow is as agreeable in Summer as it is disagreeable in Winter. There is a very grand demesne here and castle. Persons are allowed to walk in the demesne a certain number of hours each day. I avail on Sundays, and have never been as pleased, as any walk. The Blackwater runs through it, which is an addition to its charms.

Where is Clara that your cousin entered? I can't at all know. Is she named Hickey who was in mourning one time at the feast, going to the Mercy Convent? I am resolved not to tease you anymore about your vocation.

Mallow,

Sunday (undated).

How lonely you will be after the Mission by the Redemptorists…they have won the hearts of Drogheda people. All missionaries are favourites…Oblates and Passionists. I used to be crazy about them. I trust your father is getting strong, the weather since April is so fine, it would improve any delicate person…

I am getting much more contented than I was, perhaps being better used to the W's and their whims…I'm more at the millinery and machines than losing my time at sales. I would never finish my time with them…they are so cross. The old dame is 70, active, and a great businesswoman. I have arranged to pay £10 more, and leave at the end of 2 years, to get a nicer place. But don't say anything.

Mallow,

August 5ᵗʰ, 1878.

Dearest Annie,

It is the greatest shock to get a letter from my brother telling of the death of your dear and good father…I never heard until this morning…You have too much good sense to give way to an overflow of grief. Providence saw when it was best to call him away…Of all my school companions, I never cared for any other as you and your family. Such trouble, sickness and death you have had this last month. Write and let me know of Father's death. I offer you my prayers and masses and am begging you not to be fretting.

The final letter.

December 31ˢᵗ, 1878.

Dearest Annie,

Due to the hurry of business, I am late writing and trust you are not fretting, as of course, naturally, one is made feel the loss of a fond parent at this time. You ought remember, Annie, he is far better off than any one of us. Remember me to your Mamma. I will write a long letter soon. Wishing you the compliments of the Season, with fondest love, I remain,

Very sincerely yours,

L. Donor.

Original site of Donor's Green

Chapter Three
The Millextown Letters

Mary Monica Reilly was a daughter of Patrick Reilly and Dorothy (McCullough) of West Gate, Drogheda and most likely was born about 1851. Her mother died, aged 27, in June 1853, and her sister Anne in 1854, aged 2. Another sister died in 1861, aged 12 years.

In 1870, Mary Monica married Pat Reilly, Millextown, Ardee, who was a substantial farmer and landowner. He was the second son of Philip Reilly of Derrycama, and a schoolmate of Philip Callan of Philbinstown. Callan entered public life and was eventually M.P. for Co. Louth, and Pat K. Reilly was a very active supporter of his. In an election for Poor Law Guardians of Ardee Union, in March 1876, Pat Reilly headed the poll with 554 votes. William Taaffe polled in second place with 479 votes. Pat became a member of the Council of the Home Rule League and was Ardee delegate to the Irish National League in 1881.

Mary Monica commences her correspondence with Annie Moore in 1870, just prior to her marriage, and writes 150 letters, approximately 53,000 words, up to the end of 1882. The vast bulk of these come from Millextown, so I have titled them "The Millextown Letters". Mary Monica refers to Mrs. John Moore as "our Aunt" and Edward Reilly as "our Yankee cousin", which implies a step-relationship to Annie, whose grandfather had married three times.

My dearest Annie,

I am very sorry I cannot avail myself of the pleasure of accompanying you to the sea as "Uriah" has departed. I wish I could send my weary limbs with you to dear Bettystown to get a plunge. Come over on Friday without fail, and I will astonish your ears –

Your half-dead Mary.

My dear Mrs. Moore,

Father presents his compliments to you, Mr. M., and Annie and requests the pleasure of your company to dinner on Sunday at 4 o'clock.

Yours sincerely,

Mary M. O'Reilly.

West Gate, Sunday.

My dearest Annette,

Accept the enclosed with my best love. I am sorry I can send nothing worthier your acceptance, more expression of my sincere friendship for you. I cannot refrain from repeating here a simple rhyme which will explain better than I can the feelings I wish to express on St. Valentine's Day.

Accept this gift, my dearest friend,

With all the kindness I can send

And when our present gladness

Shall turn to sadness and when

The world's rough pathways

Thou hast trod, thy hopes may be

In Heaven, I trust in God.

M.M.O'R.

Hibernian Hotel,

Cork, Saturday.

My dearest Annette,

I know you will be anxious to hear of how we are progressing on our tour. I must say that I had no idea of enjoying so many beautiful scenes in so short a time. We arrived in Thurles on Tuesday evening, the next morning we set out for Killarney. We spent a few hours in Mallow. It is a delightful little place. On Wednesday evening we arrived in Killarney but don't let me begin describing it…impossible. We left yesterday *morning and arrived here at tea. We spent the day at the Cove, it surpasses anything you could imagine. We went for a sail around Spike Island and returned to Cork in time to meet the tragedian Darcy (?) Sullivan. We intend returning to Dublin this evening and will leave there for home on Wednesday, so like a dote meet us on the six train at Drogheda as Pat is very anxious to know how Joe and McC. got on. Please bring me the Argus as I would like to hear an account of the Bazaar. I had a letter from Father yesterday. Give my love to all, joined by Pat who talks in his sleep about you. Ever you fond,*

    Mary Monica O'Reilly.

P.S. Excuse the scribble as the genius is tormenting me.

Mary Monica's "delightful home", Millextown House

Millextown House,
September 22nd, 1870.

My dearest Annie,

    We arrived home safely and feel quite at home already. It would be impossible to give you an idea of our delightful home. When you visit us you will be charmed. I gave you a parcel yesterday evening – it is for Mrs. Drew – please give it to my father for her.

I expect my luggage on tomorrow if it be convenient for you to call on Miss. McQuillan and see if my things are ready and also to send me my silk with the things. I would like to have them with my luggage. Oh! Nannie! I am so very, very happy. I often think it is a dream I am hardly conscious of the reality of my being married. Write me a long, long letter and tell me how the Court affected my Drogheda friends. Give my love to all you know who I mean. Tell Ms. J. Moore I will write soon. I hardly feel like corresponding.

Ever your own,

With Pat's best love, Mary.

Millextown,
October 8ᵗʰ, 1870.

Dearest Annette,

High time to reply to your epistle. The fact is we have not yet ceased our romancing — is it not a shame? When we should be more fairly settled down to our domestic duties. Dearest you must have a very quiet time of it at Bettystown now as I am sure that it must be quite deserted. Of course you will be at West Gate on Sunday next to meet the bride (just fancy, the bride) be sure to have a full bag of news; about the Bazaar, the feeling of desolation that pervades all hearts since the departure of Miss O'Reilly. Be sure to note that also the fashions, the latest novel, music and scandal etc.

*Do you think "Lady Andlavy" (?) will be at W.G.? I hope so. I trust all the little darlings at Duleek Gate are well including my little blond friend at the big tree also baby Joe, Joe, who is I trust daily advancing in *piety* and beauty (ahem!). Mr. T Callin sends his loving remembrance — he fairly haunts Millextown to glean tidings of *you*. My darling is charming and sends his love to you, as for myself, I am almost too happy. With much love to Mamma, Father and youngsters, Believe me*

Your ever loving,

Mary M. O'Reilly.

Millextown House,
October 22ⁿᵈ, 1870.

My dearest Annie,

We got home all right on Sunday night…we intend to go to Drogheda on Thursday next (D.V.) if weather permits. If not on Friday. We will be in town about 10 o'clock as we must be home pretty early. Dearest, I must send a telegram to the Old Man who has charge of the weather and let him know that you are coming to visit me and let us have fair weather during your stay, if not the Old Fogie may look out! I have a number of letters to write and I cannot find courage to face the task. We intended visiting at the

Convent today only for it is wretchedly wet. Do not forget the children's carte; like a dote, get the receipt of the cake from Mrs. Moore for me and we will take a "spell" at it & etc.

I trust your father did not get cold on Sunday night. Give him, your Mamma, and youngsters my best love. "Skirts" sends his love to you and twenty kisses (the wretch) and … as ever your own,

Mary M. O'Reilly.

(P.S. This day 5 weeks in St. Larry's!!!!)

Millextown House,
November 12th, 1870.

My dearest Annette,

I received your welcome letter – please present our grateful thanks to your Mamma and Father for their kind invitation. We arrived home alright, the night was extremely cold. Please tell Ms. McQ. To alter my jacket…tell her to reverse the front lining and line the same as on the back and to make it to fit like a dress body. She has my pattern and to have it done by Sunday. I can get it at West Gate – make up a story to hurry her.

I trust Mrs. Edward is quite well by this time dear Annie. I will be greatly obliged if you will get me some gros grain ribbon (as much as would make a bow for my hair) the same as pattern if you cannot get it in ribbon, velvet or satin ribbon will do. I have been very lonely since you went. The weather is so cold I cannot go out much. How is your fern, I am thinking of sending some of it to the next flower show and I think we deserve a prize for discovering a new variety of fern. I hope you are all enjoying good health. We are charming. Pat joins me in sending…

Millextown,
December 19th, 1870.

My dearest Annette,

This evening my spouse gave me your "bit of writing" which I had been expecting for the last few days. I perceive by it that there are no events of importance worth relating since the birth of the hopes of the house of Curtis & Crossin. I suppose Mrs. (Oh! I forgot) Lady Andley has been in attendance on Madame Curtis. I wonder did she weep. What sympathetic Natives we are endowed with. Well to give you all the news that I am possessed of – firstly, Mr. J. Callan paid us a visit on yesterday evening. He has been studying Chesterfield's Letters and he can enter a room with such dignity as might grace a - as I don't know what.

Secondly, my Lord has been to Ardee Jail and invested in two "Grunters" (vide O'Reilly's Encyclopoedia of Bog Latin). So dear Annette, I will end my summary of interesting news after the fashion of novel writers…to amuse you, dear reader…We are looking forward to spending our first Xmas together as one of the happiest of our lives. I have every hope of it being so. Hoping to meet you again soon. With fondest love from "Skirts"…

Millextown House,
January 10ᵗʰ, 1871.

My dearest Annette,

…yesterday night. I trust my prompt reply will in some way appease your just indignation. Where do you think I have been yesterday? In Drogheda. Now don't stare. Yes Annie, and what a delightfully fine day we had too. I intended visiting that "dear" spot every day for the past fortnight, but this horrid weather prevented me, so yesterday morning it promised to be much fairer than the preceding days. Just as we were about to start a regular snow storm came on, so "a willful man must have his way" and I suppose the woman in this case has the same. When we got to West Gate I could not venture further, so you may imagine what a day I spent, we did not leave 'til 8 o'clock. I drove to Miss McQuillan's. I left my wedding dress to be altered. I have got some beautiful real black lace to put on instead of the white. She was in ecstasies with the black lace. I sent to Dublin for it. We did not pay our intended visit to that sweet city yet. Tom Neary is with us. When he is returning we will go. I heard of Mrs. Walmsley's death yesterday. I was really very sorry though I was never a great admirer of hers. So the Great McGragh has won the day. I wish him joy. I think you acted very wisely not to go to Fr. Doyle's Bazaar, for some people go there and forget the way home. Old Skins and I was delighted to hear of Martin's return for Meath. Do you know it has given the old darling the greatest ambition and courage to stand for Louth. The other morning at breakfast his imagination had so carried him off that he leapt up (at the same time nearly upsetting the table) to address the house but discovered to his grief that the learned members present were more intent on their breakfast. I paid a visit to Kate Conway – she is "up" for the French – I feel inclined to visit the Bazaar but I might as well let the Prussians into my purse as the Bazaar "pieces" (vide O'Reillys). I think it would be a rather expensive amusement.

So the Wild Healy is at last a "tied " man. Pat met Luke yesterday also the "Calico Hat", who is most anxious about my health but would not venture to meet me for the world, poor dear. I hope all Duleek Gate friends are well, don't you think I have spun a fine yarn, so

Addio with love from Skirts…

P.S. If I am forgiven, write soon.

Millextown,

December 22nd, 1872.

...*I hear that Teresa has been ill, and you have been at the Nursing*...next page marked "PRIVATE".

I do not expect to see that renowned spot (Drog.) for some time as (entre nous) I expect the arrival of an illustrious stranger one of these days and expected you would come to Millextown to be "best woman", however I cannot expect you, on account of Teresa's illness but in case of all going on well with me, you'll allow me to name you as guardian to the stranger. This is, I need not tell you, strictly private as I do not wish Mrs. M. or anyone else, to know anything until the event, for reasons I will tell you hereafter...

NOTE: Presumably this refers to the imminent arrival of her son, Patrick Kevin, who eventually came in 1873.

December 23rd, 1873.

...*I suppose you have heard of the robbery at Mr. Stoddart's...they entered through the drawing-room window and took thirty pounds out of her writing-desk (Mrs. S.) her own money and several trinkets out of her workbox, etc. He destroyed several beautiful Indian ornaments in search of money. He was arrested at Dunleer Station very comfortably seated in the carriage, en route to Dublin.*

Millextown,

Tuesday (undated, probably 1874)

My dearest Annie,

The subject of this letter will surprise you a little. I fear I cannot make it sufficiently plainer or convey to you, half of what I wish to say. Well, dear Annie, to open the case, without prejudice —

A very particular friend of ours, Mr. William Taaffe, Ardee, has spoken to us on a very important matter, he is a lovely young man without a housekeeper, companion or wife, and appears to admire your ladyship very much, and is most anxious to make your acquaintance. Pat and he intend going to Drogheda on next Wednesday, 21st inst. And have conspired to drop in to see you in a friendly way about 5 o'clock, so, unknown to the two gents, I drop you this hint.

Well, dearest Annie, of course you will be as usual neat & etc., and as a person of experience, let me to you, make yourself as pleasing as possible, as this matter is no joke and may end in a wedding. That it may is our most fervent wish and prayer. But, now of the man. He is first moral, sober, industrious and intelligent. He is respectable and well connected. His means are A1, he is without any incumbrance, and his business (drapery) is first class, and has a most comfortable home. Well, dearest Annie, if with all these, he did not possess temper and mind to make you happy, I would never mention this matter to you, but I feel confident if Mr. T. still goes forward in this matter, and that he proposes, and is accepted, that your future will be a bright and happy one. My heart is so full of prayers and wishes for you, that I can see no obstacles which may arise. I trust there may be none, but, dearest Annie, the will of God is everything and should Mr. T. ask you to be his wife, I beg of you to think seriously of it. Such a man, such a position, and such means, and such comfort will never be yours again. I write with the most sincere wishes for your happiness, such as I would write to a dear sister. I only wish I could speak to you half an hour, as I fear this letter cannot give you even an idea of the importance of this matter or of the opportunity of a happy settlement in life that is about to be offered to you.

To conclude, you will receive this "deputation" as if you were not aware of anything being in question; above all things be at your ease, or it may be suspected I gave you a hint. I wish, particularly, your Mamma to be present. You can form your plans during the day to effect this, but do not tell anyone of this letter.

I will expect a long letter from you on Thursday, and should they not go on Wednesday, you may expect them Friday or Saturday. Pat and my father are as anxious to know the results of this matter as I am. I will see you next week, without fail, with best love, dearest Annie,

Your most sincere friend, Mary M. Reilly.

Tuesday (undated)

…I will not say anything in this letter of the <u>great</u> <u>question</u> pending, except that Mr. T. was enchanted with his visit. These cursed elections will cause some delay in anything further at present. Well, Annie, I got a letter from Mrs. J. (our Aunt) and she smells a rat, so be very cautious above all…

```
WM. TAAFFE,
GENERAL DRAPERY,
WOOLLEN, MANCHESTER, & DRESSMAKING ESTABLISHMENT,
CASTLE STREET,
ARDEE.

———•———

W. T. is a Commissioner for taking Affidavits for the
High Court of Justice, and Sub-Distributor of Stamps.
```

Monday (undated)

Thank you for getting the bonnet for me — it's very pretty but the flower is not as good as I would like...

I have had two letters from Mrs. J. Moore on Saturday...mortally offended she is...then half an apology...

March 9th, 1874.

...I saw my friend, Mr. T., ...he is greatly disturbed by some unfavourable turns of the county politics. Pat and he are fearful suspicious about "The Murder" and are off to Dundalk to find the truth...all love affairs out of the question...

January 4th, 1875

...I suppose there has been ice-skating at Beaulieu. The roads about here were a perfect sheet of ice...

February 2nd, 1875

...News in this area as rare as fresh fish. I suppose the sermons etc. are the only attraction in D. — now & people are becoming devout for a change. Pat has been to fairs in Thurles and Clonmel last week — gone from Monday until Thursday night. I was perfectly miserable during the time, thinking of robbers and all kinds of accidents and misfortunes. Did you get your dress from McG. Yet? I wrote yesterday for a new

publication *"Myra's Fashions and Journal of Dress"*. She is late editoress of Beeton's…Like a dote, give me some hints on getting up a spring head gear – also kindly order from Mrs. Crilly (or whoever you get your notepaper) some cream coloured with monogram (M.M.R.)…

March 14th, 1875

…I was quite alarmed to hear about the outbreak of Fever around Duleek St.

(undated)

…I am glad to hear you have taken a place at Bettystown. I got a little sketch of your goings-on there…Who have you down there?…

June 24th, 1875

…wish to go to the seaside…searched the Northern coast and found none…my help took it into her venerable head to say she'd leave…suspend plans…found a place in Malahide, so on tomorrow, Friday, the royal family leave for the seaside…

(undated)

…Miss Reilly's fate is to be decided on next Sunday – the suitor is Mr. Dougherty of Annagassan, a very young, handsome and eligible partie, and from my heart, I pray it may take place. Of course I hear you say Oh! You are dying for a wedding, well, I am dying for all the parties that will follow. All this is <u>confidential</u>…

August 3rd, 1875

…more settled after my trip…inconvenience of lodgings…Pat is in Wicklow since Wednesday last, he was summonsed on the trial of Callan & Roe, and was not, I think, examined at all. He returns tomorrow to Dublin and remains there for the Centenary…I cannot tell you how disappointed I am at not seeing P. Reilly before his return…Could you pay for the alterations to my bonnet in Davis's shop and also a bill in Daly's, a pair of boots, I think 17/6 and a pair of stays 11/6…P.S. I enclose £2, to pay bills – M.

November 19th, 1876

My dearest Annie,

I was very sorry to hear from Pat that you have got no tidings of Johnny's ship. Mrs. J. mentioned in a postscript to me of her letter that you were very uneasy about him – that was the only intimation I got of it. I can well imagine how you all must suffer. I need not tell you I full sympathise with you…If you saw how I am situated , you would forgive and pity me. Baby is not quite as troublesome but I have the old, old story to tell of no help, I am so often changing them, that I must be looked on as a great domestic tyrant.

I got a new dress and bonnet — I do not care much for them. Pat told Mrs. Neary to send them to me, and I need not tell you regardless of expense…the dress is deep green cashmere, looks black at night with collar cuffs and pocket of silk…

Pat told me Mrs. M. was not looking at all well he thought…

We are making great alterations about the house, building a dairy, with the door opening into the kitchen, where the coals are kept, and putting up a new range, etc.

March 11ᵗʰ, 1877

My dearest Annie,

I thought you might be tempted to write to know the cause of my silence — those foolish promises I make of writing first and having nothing to say except the death of some old woman or some of those romantic marriages that are so common about this place. I hope Maggie is getting better — every day I intend to write, and like all my good intentions, the writing gets forgotten about. When you write tell me all about her.

We left West Gate very soon after you went. I was obliged to use my authority to get my Lord away, Mon Pere was quite offended when I offered any objection to his staying there till morning. Now, Annie dear, is it any wonder that I should dislike going to West Gate? I am still depressed after my last visit. I heard a very bad account of "the goings-on" at W.G. a few days ago. Should you hear anything fresh, let me know. We are all quite well here and unite in best love…write soon…

Mary M. O'Reilly.

(undated)

P.S. A word about myself — I am much more genteel than when you saw me last and very strong T.G. News from West Gate is anything but cheerful — I often say "Thank God — all my troubles come from that quarter". They can't be eternal. Have you wondered at the baby's name? Or did you hear it? Edmund Richard Vincent. Why we called him so, I can't tell. I never gave the name a thought, until he arrived — I was so confident of not having another mischiefmaker!

Millextown,
July 3ʳᵈ, 1877

I am just in the humour of writing a long epistle…I was in Dublin on Thursday week and invested in a drab cashmere dress, Princess of course. I think it very pretty and you know the pleasure of liking a dress is everything. We went again on Friday, and took the boys — went to the Zoological Gardens and tea. They were delighted — the day was very wet…We spent the evening in Mrs. Neary's. I must wait until we meet to give you an account of the conduct of these three "enfants terrible"! We were at a dinner party in S_____ on

Sunday week. Nearly all quiet married people. It was a most gloomy affair! I have just read Dickens' "Great Expectations" and am delighted with it…

Millextown,

August 12th.

You will be sorry to hear I have been very ill for about a fortnight. Dr. Moore has been with me several times – I am able to be up and no more – he says I am to keep perfectly quiet for the next two weeks before he can say I am out of danger. Joseph and Pat are now quite recovered from the Measles – Dilly and baby are just laid up but going on well. I am very sorry to hear Mrs. Moore has not improved lately – I was most anxious to see her…My father heard of my illness, but never wrote a line to know how I was. I fear it will be some time before I can go to Drogheda.

Miss Marry's, Balbriggan

October 5th, 1877

Dearest Annie,

You will be very surprised to hear that I am sojourning in this out of the way place – I took the notion of going to the sea quite suddenly and I am very glad I came…the weather is delightful, the place very amusing and mine hostess very agreeable. Kate Reilly is stopping in the same house…I came on Monday and intend to return on Monday week. M.M. Devine, your friend of the Bazaar is staying next door…

I hope you got home safely after escorting me to the terminus, I did, but was very cross with that Home Ruler for his very gushing manner to you on the platform. It's time to ask you how you liked Dalkey…

Millextown,

November 11th, 1877

…Pat has gone to a fair in Charleville, Co. Cork…our visit to Dublin has to be put off. The programme I have arranged for our visit (it is understood that you are to come!). I intend our visit to be a pleasure as I have very little shopping to do. 1st, a visit of condolence to Mrs. Neary – I suppose you have heard of the death of one of her children. 2nd, carte taken, 3rd, skating rink, look at shop windows (my delight) then we will finish up with the theatre. I would not think of returning the same day, as they are so very short now. The next day we will do our shopping etc., and then I hope you will return to Millextown.

December 23rd, 1877

…I am very glad to have one I know – I really do not know how to thank you for your kindness to the boys. Pat is delighted. You would not really think it was Xmas in the country at all except the droves of

poor people coming for the last week. We expect J. Kearns tomorrow…My Lord says it is post time, so I must conclude…

January 13th, 1878

…I had a dreadful time of it since, because for the last ten days, the four children were very ill. Baby had a very severe attack of croup on last Wednesday week, and I did not expect baby to recover – the Doctor is taking great credit for himself over the case. All the children around here have whooping cough…

I believe P. Callan had a very quiet wedding…I am very curious to see the bride.

May 5th, 1878

…I had a letter from your Aunt M. yesterday, she told me about Maggie Healy's romantic adventure. I can hardly believe it, even yet. Pat says she is a plucky girl. I think it would be a very unsuitable marriage. I am in great trouble over a bonnet (nothing new for me!)…

June 9th, 1878

…Pat is very much better, but cannot leave the sofa all day. His knee is healing but he cannot use his leg at all yet. I have not left the house except to go to Mass since the accident happened…I am sorry to hear that Mrs. Moore has been ill…she was to have a table at the Bazaar and feels very nervous about it, but depends very much on your bringing her through the ordeal.

June 29th, 1878

…Pat went to Mass today for the first time since his accident…I heard my father was ill but got no particulars – I suppose it is the old story, with him again. Mrs. Moore told me she is still on the sick list and had been to Dublin…she is now a long time in delicate health. Did you get anything new in the dress line – tell me when you write…

July 5th, 1878

My dearest Annie,

I cannot tell you how shocked and grieved we were to hear of your dear father's death. I can well imagine your grief. May God comfort you all. I am in some affliction about Pat, his leg burst in a fresh place last night and he is in great pain. He is completely laid up again. I cannot write any more or the half of what I feel. As ever,

Mary.

William Forde,

FAMILY GROCER,
TEA, WINE, AND SPIRIT MERCHANT,
10 SHOP STREET,
DROGHEDA.

HENRY McCULLEN,
BUILDER AND CONTRACTOR,
JOHN STREET,
DROGHEDA.

Building materials of every description always in stock.   All kinds
of carpenter work done in the best manner, and upon the cheapest terms.
Funeral requisites supplied on the shortest notice.

Mrs. RICHARD MOORE,
TEA, WINE, SPIRIT & PROVISION MERCHANT,

DULEEK GATE,
DROGHEDA.

EDWARD McDONNELL,
FAMILY GROCER, WINE AND SPIRIT MERCHANT,
52 LAURENCE STREET, DROGHEDA.

Teas, Coffees, Brandies, Wines, John Jameson and Son's Old
Whiskey, Bass & Co.'s Pale Ales, Guinness's Double Stout, Wax &
Composite Candles, &c., &c.

Advertisements from Basset's Co. Louth Directory,

published 1886

July 29th, 1878

My dearest Annie,

    I have been so much engaged with this latest arrival I had not time to write…I am almost quite recovered, though a perfect skeleton, skin and bone, I hardly know myself when I look in the glass. The baby is a fine little fellow – his name is Charles Miles – poor fellow he got a cool reception for being a boy, I am the only one in the house decently civil to him. Pat is getting on very slowly – this hot weather is greatly against healing…

September 8th, 1878

    …I am constantly occupied with baby alone – he sleeps very little during the day…We intend to go to Drogheda next Sunday to hear Fr. Burke's sermon, when I hope to see you all.

    Pat is dining with Fr. Levins today – it is the patron saint's day of this parish. I heard Fr. O'Reilly was at home for some time and had as usual not seen him – it is four years since we met. I hope dear Annie you feel stronger – you should go out as often as you can…

November 24th, 1878

    …Were you fortunate at the Bazaar? I believe some of the prizes were dearly paid for in much arrogance, as well as coin of the realm…I am longing to hear particulars from you…I want a dress and some kind of headgear very badly. I would rather go to Dublin but the days are so short for shopping.

    I fear the boys are about to lose Miss Mathews – she is promised a school and intends to go…

December 30th, 1878

    …I dread a repetition of what I got at Xmas Day and the two following days from Mon Pere – such a temper as it was in, all over the balance of trade etc.,…such croaking I hope I shall never hear again. Old '78 is dying fast and I think it will be long remembered as a sad year.

February 23rd, 1879

    …I have something wonderful, which seldom happens me. I suppose you saw the announcement of Miss Neary's marriage in the Freeman. I got a letter from her a few days before telling me she was to be married on the 15th, Saturday morning at 8 o'clock, strictly private, then after dejeuner they were to start for Killarney…I never got a bit of the cake, if such a thing is now in fashion, all the pleasant good old fun of putting a scrap in our stocking to dream on is gone…

March 19th, 1879

    Thanks for your nice long letter, I wonder you did not hear from your Aunt in that Pat has scarlatina – three weeks confined upstairs…I never went out, not even to Mass…I am so glad you got a machine…*you will find it great to make your underclothing etc. Last year all I paid for sewing for myself, children and household was four shillings.*

I believe the Empress has returned to Austria this week so I cannot have the pleasure of seeing her…

April 14th, 1879

You will be sorry to hear that Dilly has been very ill for three weeks. Early this week the scarlatina took a typhoid form. The Doctor had little hope for a fortnight – he is now able to sit up in bed. T.G. Pat is quite strong again – his illness made him as bold and impudent as possible.

My father did not pay his Easter visit to us – he said he was strongly advised not to go to Millextown for fear of catching the sickness. "Good people are scarce!"

Tuesday (undated)

…I shall go to 12 o'clock mass at the Dominicans and then to Robinsons – could you meet me at either place? So that we could have a long day…

Wednesday (undated)

I see you have not heard of our troubles. Poor little Edmund is dying. He got diptheria after scarlatina. Drs. Moore & Callan say there is no hope. Dr. Moore says it would be cruel to give us any hope. The baby got over it in a few days and Dilly (Philip) is quite well.

My father was anointed on Thursday – he is better now. Dearest, ask all the prayers you can for us. WE are worn out. I never knew sorrow before.

As ever, with best love,

Mary.

June 1st, 1879

Thank you for all your kindness and letters – I could not write a line, I feel so sad, and miss my pet, more every day. While your Mamma was with me, chatting to her kept me up, but then when she left, I cannot tell you how lonely I got.

I intend to send Joe and Pat to school tomorrow – Dilly and baby are quite well.

July 4th, 1879

…I have not been at all well, and to add to my misery, I have been tormented with toothache since Sunday…Maggie's death after all was a surprise to me…I am very miserable and unhappy about my father's affairs – he is giving us great trouble.

P.S. I left the collars and some pictures for you at Miss McQuillan's.

July 23rd, 1879

...*face very swollen – I am afraid I must have a tooth drawn – there is a tumour gathering in my gum...plans to take the boys to Annagassan races but Joe got measles – he is ill since Sunday...Mon Pere is very offended if I spend much time in your locality...*

Pat Reilly of West Gate died September 4th, 1879 and is buried in the Cord Cemetery, Drogheda.

REILLY

Erected 1853 by Patrick Reilly of West Gate, Drogheda in memory of his wife Dorothy who died 13th June 1853 aged 27 years. Also her daughters Anne who died 8th May 1854 aged two years and Bridget who died 23rd November 1861 aged 12 years. Also to the memory of his mother-in-law Mary McCullough who died 17th December 1868 aged 70 years. Of your Charity pray for the happy repose of the soul of the above Patrick Reilly who died 4th September 1879 aged 67 years.

The letters from this date until December 1880 are on notepaper with black edging.

November 7th, 1879

...*I have been in Dublin to see Miss Bateman as Mary Warner – I enjoyed the play very much, I will tell you all about it when I see you...a good many purchases for the boys...returned with a very light purse! I suppose you are enjoying yourself on the ice...*

November 9th, 1879

...*I want to give you "a bit of my mind" <u>concerning yourself</u>. It's not enough to compare me to Mrs. Langan, and to go about visiting in all directions and telling me you can't go any place but you must never write me a line this three months. You are really changed and I am getting terribly jealous of two persons. I tell you the rest when I see you.*

December 21st, 1879

I am requested by your precious Godson to thank you very much for your kind present. He made several efforts to do so today but was not satisfied with the result – it was so kind and thoughtful of you...I feel very sad at the approach of Xmas, our small circle will be smaller still...About the hat, if it is ready on Saturday, it will be soon enough...

February 8th, 1880

...I am quite terrified at the approach of Lent – I must only play the invalid and claim a little indulgence. Did the Ball come off in Drogheda – I heard nothing of it since. There is not a scrap of news in the country. Pat is dining this evening with P. McGee, only the lords of creation and the Party (that they may be sick tomorrow). Is that not too bad? I had a second letter from Mrs. Daly asking £1 to help buy a chalice and vestments for the Chord Chapel...

April 8th, 1880

My dearest Annie,

I am in such bad humour since the election began I could not write to you. Pat is from home every day for the last week and so many calling I am in dreadful humour. I had just commenced my Spring housecleaning when the annoyance came. Mrs. Callan is very busy canvassing and displays the London fashions to the envy and admiration of the County – she is looking very worn and careworn. The people in Ardee are like lunatics fighting and bawling and abusing each other...Please get me the book from the Convent you were speaking about. I suppose you have Richie at home yet – he must be highly amused at the election proceedings.

P.S. Pat's leg is going on very badly. I am sure he will be laid up after the exertions – I am very miserable about it. The boys are very well.

M.

April 18th, 1880

...I went to Drogheda in the outside car and got such a wetting...We were in Dublin on Monday and (very fortunately) were late for the last train. We went to the Gaiety – the play was not very good. Mrs. Callan called on Monday so I had not the pleasure? Of seeing her. I left my silk jacket with Miss McQuillan to make some alterations...

Mrs. Morgan's
Seabank
Castlebellingham.
June 22nd, 1880

We arrived on Tuesday – the boys are delighted and no end of trouble...they are at present in bed (10 o'clock) doing penance for swimming in their clothes. This day is intensely warm – I will collect you on Sunday at Drumleck Station at half past twelve train. I will tell you all about the profession when we meet...

July 1^{*st*}*, 1880*

Seabank.

I felt quite disappointed when I got your letter – of course you are keeping yourself fresh for Bellewstown, and would not risk your complexion at the seaside. Have the pilgrims returned from Knock?…We went to the Black Rocks on Tuesday, it is a very cheerful place, with as many people as Bettystown on a Sunday and a band playing. I am quite copper coloured and the boys in rags – I wish there was some pawn shop near that I could get them some clothes…

Millextown,

Friday (undated)

I send you some cuttings of geraniums as you have plenty of space you might plant them all - some will grow – they are nearly all different colours. I tried to get some pelagoniums from Paddy Branagan but did not succeed…The boys are about to make an attack on the nuts and apples so I must conclude…

August 20^{*th*}*, 1880*

…Pat commenced reaping today – he will be very busy for some time. The weather is all they can wish for.

My father's anniversary will take place on Wednesday next, mass at 10 o'clock. I hope you got the books alright. I suppose Patrick returned to Tullabeg next day. He is not the least changed in his manner. Should you come to the mass, please bring the bills for dying my dress, as I am settling my affairs. I fear May's property suffered from the boys' visit. I told them they were like little hungry pigs – they were not much offended.

October 25^{*th*}*, 1880*

I was getting quite alarmed about you until I got your letter – so many rash young men from this part of the country wandering about town and no one to look after them. I was delighted to hear the Bazaar was such a success. Did you win many prizes?

I am just beginning to stir about again and feel very well and strong (T.G.). Baby (Dorothea) is going on splendidly. Joseph is the only one who seems to care about her. I am glad Sissy has gone to Daly's…

November 11^{*th*}*, 1880*

Your letter puzzled me so much I don't know how to begin to write and to congratulate you. Of course I must when you say you are so happy. Is it the ring or the veil? Twenty times in the day, I ask myself – "Who is he?" Well Annie, you <u>can</u> keep a secret. I must contrive to see you soon…

December 5th, 1880

I got home alright and found the baby did not miss me in the least…Pat was very glad to hear all the good news…you may expect a good quizzing when he sees you. I had a great treat on Thursday – a certain Mrs. Murphy, who sells underclothing for the Sisters of Mercy, Newry, called and showed me her stock. The needlework was most beautiful and the make of the different articles quite new to me. Pat bought some shirts and paid pretty smart for them too. I made a few purchases for her ladyship – such lovely little bibs! Here's a wrinkle for you – all the best things she had were trimmed with Troscan lace, it is quite yellow but very nice and good. I ordered a knitted petticoat from her, the Nuns pray for anyone giving an order…

February 7th, 1881

…I hope the young gentleman is quite well. I expect he is beginning to notice you already. Perhaps I will take a run out to see you on Saturday. Pat has gone to the fair of Kilkenny and will not be back until Thursday. We had a great day on Saturday last in Dublin. We took the boys to the pantomime. They were delighted with the performance especially the comic business. I did not care much for it, the midday performance is seldom good. I did very little shopping. How is Papa McC. progressing with the nursing? I intend to argue that point with him very soon. Give him my kindest regards.

July 3rd, 1881

…If it ever happens again, I may say with truth you have quite forgotten me. It would be hard indeed if I were to lose your dear welcome letter. I had my drawing room painted and bought the carpet for it; now begins the great work of furnishing. …very busy with my turkeys and ducks, etc. They are nearly as troublesome as babies. I suppose you intend to go to Bellewstown; don't let Mr. McCullen go alone – some of his old flames might run away with him, and poor Annie would be quite forlorn. Dora is getting to be a very fine girl…

August 1st, 1881

…the pleasure of seeing you and Pat in Millextown…put off by many things…the pleasure of dining with us next Sunday. We intended giving you a grand party on your marriage but Pat is so downcast at present I gave up on the idea, as it looked so much out of place any rejoicing and he is in so much trouble about the cattle. I am sorry to tell you that they are still affected, even the milch cows – two died…

Kindest regards to you and Pat (I will call him the familiar name, being his <u>senior</u>)…

October 14th, 1881

…streets were a perfect sea…sent James to the Chord to plant some flowers on the grave. I left some snow-drop bulbs at West Gate to be sent to you…

Did you know of the great meeting to be held in Ardee on Sunday next? I am getting quite nervous about my Leaguer – it's well your good man is not rebelliously inclined. Now, Madam, your last letter was very short…the only way to have a good long chat would be by going to town on the train, and then direct to Greenore!

Millextown,

Monday (undated)

…I am very uneasy about your dress. Pat called to Langan's last Thursday week and they said you got it, and left another to be dyed…I went to the Pantomime on Thursday night. It is in my opinion, a spectacle not fit for anyone only inmates of a lunatic asylum, nothing but tinsel, lights and legs (and by the way, a little too much of the latter to be seen). I thought the music very poor indeed. The latest in Drogheda is P. Long's marriage – I must say he is the only one who kept up the credit of your locality before Lent.

November 17th, 1881

I shall leave the patterns we were speaking about in Duleek St., and a little egg basket which you are to gather the full of every day.

I think our Leaguers are safe. I heard that there are new beds put up in Dundalk Jail yesterday. I hope there is none of them for our poor Pats – they would feel very cold to spend their Xmas. I hope you are taking great care of yourself and not racing about…

Friday (undated)

…I have just finished "Oliver Twist" and am delighted with it…

Undated

...we intend to go to the Regatta at Skerries tomorrow – Mr. Healy invited us to spend the day with him...

December 22nd, 1881

I have just got Lizzie's welcome letter with the good news. We all send congratulations to you both, on the arrival of the little Xmas visitor...Be wise enough to take care of yourself, this cold weather. My first visit will be to see your dear boy. ..Pat says he will give some lessons in nursing to P.McC...he considers himself perfect in the art.

January 17th, 1882

...I hope the young man is conducting himself peaceably. I suppose you saw in "the Argus" about Mrs. McGee's son – he is a remarkably fine child and she is very strong already. Of course there is great joy...Glad to tell you that Pat's eye is almost well and he can raise the eyelid...

Has Papa McCullen nursed his son yet? I think he does when no one is watching...

Tuesday (undated)

...I intend to get baby vaccinated one of these days. I believe I am a law-breaker not having the operation performed before this. We are to have several marriages early in June.

Mr. T. McGee (brother of P. McGee) to Miss Durnin. Mr. Halpenny to Miss Stein, Mandistown and P. Callan (Shanlis), widower, to Miss Fitzsimons...

I think I shall drop into Beamore some fine day soon, for a long chat.

March 17th, 1882

You must think me very lazy...I feel quite strong T.G. and got over my illness quite quickly. Baby (Mary Monica) is a fine strong girl, my namesake, and is pronounced already "my very likeness". I suppose your boy is haymaking these days...I need not ask for your good man, I am told he is becoming a second Tichbourne...

August 20th, 1882

...the baby is rather troublesome, and takes up a great deal of my time...I am glad to hear your baby has got his first grinder, it is an important event, with nurses at least...I hope to take a few drives to the sea, as soon as I can...I trust your good man is quite well.

November 12th, 1882

A nice way I have kept my promise of writing soon...pressure of business – we visited the Exhibition on Monday and took the boys including Charlie. They enjoyed it very much. If you and I were there comparing notes, I would have enjoyed it ever so much more...

I intend to consult Dr. Moore tomorrow about this ornamentation on my head, I fancy it's getting larger each day. I intend to have your Mother's opinion also, that will be the final one, then for action…

I need not enquire for the big man – I know he is quite well…

Millextown,
December 23rd, 1882

My dearest Annie,

I have been every day intending to write to you, but so busy, so sick and <u>so cross</u>. I let old father Christmas nearly in the door before doing so. I went to Drogheda about three weeks ago intending to pay a visit to your Mother. The day turned out very wet and I am only alive since. I am fretting very much about the wen on my head, for the last few days I feel it very painful, it is larger since you saw it. I don't like going to Dr. Moore, his wife is dying and he is poorly himself.

I was expecting a letter from you long since to tell me all about M. Hickey's marriage. I suppose the lassies had a fine time of it. Poor Annie and poor me, we are laid on the shelf. Well every dog has his day, that's a comfort. Pat and the young folk got over the severe weather very well. I trust your good man and the dear boy are quite well. All unite with me in wishing you, Pat and the little man a most happy Christmas and many bright returns of the New Year, and

With best love, believe me,

Dearest Annie,

As ever, M.M. Reilly.

At the time of writing this December 1882 letter, Mary Monica has had five sons and two daughters in twelve years, one son Edmund, has died aged three, and her father has also passed on.

After 1882, six more children came along giving a total of thirteen:

Joseph Malachy (1871)	Sponsors: Patk. McGee & Mary Steen
Patk. Kevin (1873)	Sponsors: Thomas Neary & Anne Moore
Philip Gerald (1874) "Dilly"	Sponsors: Pat Reilly & Anne Moore
Edmund Michael (1876)	Sponsors: Laurence Healy & Kate Reilly

Charles Myles (1878)	Sponsors: Mat Reilly & Mary A. Kelly
Dorothea Mary (1880)	Sponsors: Patrick Duffy & Mary J. Moore
Mary Monica (1882)	Sponsors: Jos. Mal. Reilly & Mary Duffy
Agnes Mary (1883)	Sponsors: Patk. K. Reilly & Julia Reilly
Eileen Mary (1885)	Sponsors: Edward O'Reilly & Mary Moore
Frances Josephine (1887)	Sponsors: Philip Reilly & Mary Malone
Myles William (1888)	Sponsors: Patk. Reilly & Maggie Duffy
Maurice Edmund (1889)	Sponsors: Chas. Myles Reilly & _____
Gerald Aloysius (1891)	Sponsors: Thomas Callan & Dorothy M. Reilly

Mary Monica died in 1899 on September 4th, at the age of 48 and is buried in plot 149, in Ballapousta Cemetery. Her eldest daughter Dora died in 1900 aged 20 years, and Pat Reilly was himself buried in September 1911. A small semi-circular headstone marks the burial place of all three. The Millextown property passed to Joseph Reilly, a grandson of Pat and Mary, who had a solicitor's practice in Drogheda, and lived at Weir Hope House, Marsh Road. His practice ceased about the middle of the 1950s and he threw his energies into Louth G.A.A. affairs, where he was County Board Chairman for many years. His eldest son Joe was a classmate of my own at St. Joseph's C.B.S., in Drogheda, and after doing his Leaving Certificate in 1958, joined the U.S. Air Force, and was killed in an accident in the U.S.

While we were at school together in the 1950s, my Aunt Mary would often question me about the welfare of Joe Reilly. Now I have some idea of why she took such an interest in the great grandson of her mother's best friend...

Joe the Solicitor / G.A.A. man had a large family, some of whom are still living around this area and I was made most welcome by another descendant of Mary Monica – Diana McCarthy-Lynch, who has a shop on the Main Street in Ardee. When M.M.R. died in 1899, several of the Reilly children were sent to other related families in County Louth, to be reared, according to Arthur McKevett of Kilkerly, whose grandmother was a Reilly.

"We have loved her in life, let us
not forget her in death."

Sweet Sacred Heart of Jesus,

Have mercy on the Soul of

MARY MONICA REILLY,

MILLEXTOWN, ARDEE.

Who died the 3rd September, 1899,

R.I.P.

If love and care could death prevent,
Thy days would not so soon be spent;
Life was desired, but God did see,
Eternal life was best for thee,

Chapter Four
The Lives of Reilly

"The Bull of Brooklyn"

While Mary Monica Reilly (nee Reilly) on some occasions refers to Annie Moore as "cousin", the exact genealogical relationship is not yet clear. An examination of the Moore accounts for 1856 reveals that Patt Reilly of West gate was a substantial customer of Richard Moore, and also got four bottles of brandy on August 26th, 1856. In Chapter One, we mentioned the fact that Richard Moore Senior was a child of a thrice-married Father. This man's name was John, and his first marriage produced two sons and four daughters, whom we can call the Carrantown Moores, because this is where they were based for well over a century, half way between Drogheda and Duleek. The second marriage produced Richard and John, both of who had shops in Duleek Street, and this branch can be called the Duleek Gate family. John went on to marry a third wife, named Mary Hickey, and had six children with her, three boys and three girls, and they lived at Kellystown, Donore – the Kellystown Moores. One of those girls, named Mary, in 1859 married Edward Reilly, of Coolagh Street and in turn, had a family of three boys and three girls. Two of the sons and two of the daughters emigrated to America, as did two of their aunts, and one son, Edward, became a household name in 1935.

Original home of Edward Reilly at 68, Coolagh Street
(afterwards Thorntons, and now site of the garden of John and Marie McGovern)

Edward J. Reilly

Edward J. Reilly studied law in New York and was a very successful lawyer, gaining the name of "the Bull of Brooklyn" because of his loud, theatrical style as a defence attorney. He mixed in influential political circles, and was adept at using friends in the Press in order to build campaigns on behalf of his clients. By 1935, an addiction to alcohol, particularly Martinis for lunch, had reduced his effectiveness, and a string of lost cases gained him the new nickname, "Death House Reilly". Most of his clients went to the electric chair at this stage. He was hired by the Hearst Corporation to add colour to the trial of Richard "Bruno" Hauptmann, who was accused of being the kidnapper and murderer of the baby son of Charles and Anne Lindbergh. The child's name was also Charles, although, at two years old, he was already nicknamed "the Little Eagle".

Lindbergh became a world celebrity in May 1927 when he flew his plane " The Spirit of St. Louis" in the first transatlantic flight from Long Island USA to Paris France. When he married the daughter of the American Ambassador to Mexico in 1929, they immediately became a couple that the Press loved to follow. Anne, in her own right, was the author of several best selling books.

Their first child was little Charlie who was born in June 1930. The kidnapping took place on February 27th 1932 and a demand was made for $50,000. The ransom was paid but the child was not returned because the kidnapper had broken the ladder to the window and fallen to the ground killing the baby. He then panicked and buried the body a few miles from the house. Seventy-two days later, the body was found and the hunt for the murderer intensified. By following the manufacture of the broken ladder, the police eventually arrested Richard "Bruno" Hauptmann on September 19th 1934.

The trial of Hauptmann commenced in Flemington, New Jersey, On January 2nd 1935, and lasted for 32 days, during which Edward Reilly was at the center of the drama, but was not very successful in building a credible defence for his client. There were disagreements between members of the defence team and accusations that Edward Reilly really believed his client was guilty of the crime, and had only spent a total of forty minutes talking with Hauptmann. After the verdict, while the appeal was being prepared, Reilly withdrew from the case, accused of demanding money from his client, but saying that his real reason was a publicity drive by supporters of Hauptmann to collect money for a defence fund. Their methods used a racist theme of Jew versus German and Reilly objected to this.

A jury found Hauptmann guilty of "murder in the first degree". The intrusion of the Press, and also threats of another child kidnap, eventually forced the Lindberghs to leave the U.S. and settle in England, in January 1936. Several stays of execution were placed on Hauptmann's sentence, but he eventually died in the electric chair on April 3rd 1936. Edward Reilly suffering from syphillis and a nervous breakdown entered a psychiatric hospital in the autumn of 1935, a long distance from his origins in Duleek Gate.

Amongst others involved in the case was Al Capone who was in prison at the time, but offered to find the kidnappers if he were allowed out of jail. Lindbergh refused the offer. Colonel Norman Schwarzkopf was Superintendant of the N.J. State Police and was a very important member of the investigation team. His son of the same name was the "Stormin' Norman" of the Gulf War.

A "Combination" Harvester and Thresher at work in Montana.

Apart from the Reilly connection with America, there were several other Moores, McCullens, Taaffes and Hickeys who had emigrated to the "Land of the Free". A postcard of September 1910 from one of these, J.P. Moore, shows a huge combine harvester at work, and advises Pat McCullen to come out and see the way to do the grain harvest, in Butte, Montana. There is more Moore in a letter from Annie to Richard.

September 28ᵗʰ, 1909

My dear R.

...We received a large photo from the Yanks in Butte, it is a life like group of Pa and Ma, two sons and two daughters...

There may be somebody descended from Pa and Ma out there, so I publish the photo, which was framed and kept in Beamore for almost a century.

The Yanks from Butte, J.P. Moore and family, 1909

" The Mysterious Cousin"

Some years ago after sifting through old letters before the appearance of Monica's writings, I came across a letter headed *St. Vincent's Home, Queen's Rd., Hull* dated 14th Oct, 1939 and addressed to my father at the time of his wedding. It reads –

My dear Cousin,

Please accept the sincere congratulations of your old cousin, may yourself and your dear Bride live long to enjoy many happy returns of the anniversary of your wedding day. God send you good luck and every happiness. I enjoyed your lovely cake sent to me by your dear sister. It brought back many memories of you all, and your dear Father and Mother R.I.P. who after their wedding were better known for many years as "Here comes Pat and the Bride, God bless them".

May He bless you both in your new life and give you good health, to enjoy many happy and prosperous years together. This is the sincere wish of

Your fond cousin in J.C.,
Sister Mary Reilly, Sister of Charity.

As I put the letter to one side, I wondered who on earth this nun was and where the "Reilly" came from. Waiting for some piece of information to come from somewhere, for twenty years, I thought that the trail was growing colder after quizzing my cousins who were over eighty years of age, and drawing a blank. One day in 2001, I mentioned it to Fr. Dick McCullen, a younger relation, and within days he came back with an article from an Irish Vincentian publication called "Colloque". It is written by Sr. Judith Greville, D.C., Archivist of the British Province of the Order, and her intention is to focus on the style of directorship of the Daughters of Charity at the time. I am reproducing the piece in full because it refers to the "fond cousin" of my father, who was in fact, his first step-cousin, once removed, and also the sister of Edward "Death House" Reilly.

The Life, (and Death) of Reilly !
Judith Greville DC

One of the areas of ministry about which little enough has been written is that of the directorship of the Daughters of Charity, Sr. Judith Greville DC , archivist of the British province, gives an interesting sidelight in this account of a *style* of directorship now no longer in operation.

Some thoughts on the life - and, especially, the afterlife - of Sr. Mary Francis Reilly
1871-1949

The Daughters made their first foundation in Ireland at Drogheda. It opened on 8th November 1853 as an industrial school. On 4th October 1871, Mary Francis Reilly was born in that town, daughter of Edward and Mary Reilly (variously spelt Reilly and O'Reilly) and baptised the following day in St.Marys Church. It may well be that she attended the school for she subsequently entered the Community and postulated there, arriving at the Seminary on the 10th January 1894. Her Seminary Notes were not particularly notable:

Tall. Character good and simple. Not much energy but has a free and unconstrained spirit. Judgement and intelligence ordinary. Submissive, laborious and pious. Not much education (let us hope this does not reflect on the school!).

She received the habit in August on the same year and was placed in Central House, Mill Hill.

Like most sisters she served in several houses: 1897 Smyllum Parke Orphanage, Lanark; 1904 Gainford,Co. Durham; 1910 Hull, 1934 Gravesend and 1936 at St Vincents Boys Home in Hull where she was Sister Servant. She died in 20th November 1949 and was buried in the Holderness Road Cemetery, Hull.

Again, like most sisters, her brief notes say little about her life and achievements or that inner life known to God alone . She left no   biography or diaries. She was really very ordinary and unremarkable. She did her work adequately. She does not appear as a "notable other" in any classification. Except that is until November 1951 when the local authorities decided to relocate the cemetery. Permission was granted to exhume the graves and the Community received the following letter from H Moses & Sons, Funeral Furnishers of Beverly Road, Hull.

21 December 1951

To whom it may concern,
I was present at the Exhumation of the late Sister Mary Frances (Reilly) on the 16th November 1951 and am able to state that the body was intact and easily recognisable , being in a remarkable state of preservation.
Signed A Harold Moses
Managing Director, H Moses & Sons Ltd

Some sisters who were young in the community around this time remembered being told that a sister had been found incorrupt. It was no big deal, but came out as a yarn at recreation time – more by way of amusement at the reaction of the then Director than as a pious reflection on the sister concerned! It was said that a sister came flying into the chapel to tell Fr Joe Sheedy the news and found him saying his office. ' Father, they have just found a sister in the Hull cemetery whose body is incorrupt'. It is reported that he did not look up from his breviary but said "We have plenty of saints in our Community. Sister. Bury her !"

Fortunately the sisters did begin to ask what Sister Mary Francis Reilly was really like. We have two accounts of her. One of these accounts is undated, but the other was written on 27th February 1952. We treasure them. Here they are in full:

Re Sister Reilly who was found incorrupt when the coffin was opened.

A Sister writes – When I came to Mill Hill in 1895 Sr. Reilly had charge of the kitchen, after receiving the Holy Habit . A tall slim sister, very laborious and a very capable manager, her office always in perfect order. She was gifted by God with the greatest favour of making Community Life happy for herself and others, by a great sense of humour, and hence was always bright and smiling no matter what happened. She enjoyed telling us that in Phibsborough where she lived before entering, old Fr. Dan O Sullivan had his confessional there. Once an evening she went to him. In those days no such thing as electric light was in common use, and Fr Dan kept a lighted candle in the box. Seeing him bringing it towards her face she blew it out, vigorously ! That was typical of what she would do, and enjoy doing.

All her Community life was spent in kitchens, and was cooking her best. She took pleasure and interest in it. The kitchen was a hive of industry in those days. The Seminary Sisters helped her at work there, scrubbing and rubbing. There were no aids in use to lessen the labour anywhere about the house. After two years of such activity, in her zeal to be always first down in the morning after the rising bell at 4 o'clock she suffered an unfortunate mishap. She had placed her cornette overnight on top of her jug, not noticing that it was full to the brim with water that had soaked it…It was only later on in the morning that she realised the fact. It had serious results, causing her to become deaf with ear inflammation. She was moved from Mill Hill and never placed there again, but she was devoted to Central House and always came there for her retreats. Sister Langdale laughingly said that she was so delighted to be there again that she herself nearly lost her balance through the vigorous clutch she received on her arrival.

After working in the various kitchens in the Province she came to Gravesend. When visiting her kitchen there it was indeed edifying to see how devoted she was to keeping Our Lords words in her heart. I was hungry and you gave me to eat. Such was the care she had for the poor. At this point of her life she became delicate, but was always up for the morning Mass. To attain this she so arranged her work that all food for the household's supper and breakfast was prepared perfectly before she retired to bed about 4 o'clock. This was her custom during the rest of her stay at Gravesend. Her kitchen labours ended when she was made Sister Servant in Hull. When I took her up there she laughingly said 'Glory be to God, to think of taking the old rooster from her perch to make her a sister servant!'

The people up there took to her bright and kindly ways and she was devoted to the Poor. The Rev Fr. Mackin was the Parish Priest at the time, but not for very long as he went over to Ireland and died rather suddenly there. Sister was extremely good to priests and big-hearted to everyone. When the late War broke out the household moved for safety up to Scarborough.

Her letters which always ended with 'God and Mary bless you! ' were full of admiration of the beautiful scenery up there. She was always wishing to be moved from the office of Sister Servant, saying she should never have been made one. It was characteristic of her not to blame companions who had various ways "unlike what sisters ought to have". Her way of describing them was simply to laugh and say, 'isn't it funny that sisters should have got into such queer ways? Sister Branningan, who was moved from the orphanage there, was alone with her at the moment of her death as the sisters were at Mass, and could give the best details of what it was like. Sister Reilly could not be left alone for any length of time, her heart being so affected.
Signed Sister Josephine O'Driscoll.

Sister Margaret Branigan wrote as follows

My dear Sister Augustine,
The Grace of our Lord be with us for ever!
Your surely did spring a surprise on me with your letter about Sister Mary RIP. As Sister was very ill when I arrived and remained so till her death, there isn't very much I can say. As a matter of fact too, her mind was affected so we had a job coping with her, as you will remember she was a big and masterful woman.

One thing I did notice she was a great prayer. She had great devotion to ejaculatory prayers, and would be heard repeating them many times during the days and nights. Sister retained her strong sense of humour and repartee right up to the last. From many who attended her funeral I gathered that Sister was famous in Hull for all her embracing charity and kindness, particularly to the boys of the "Working Boys Home" where she had laboured for many years.

The presence too, of the Bishop and over thirty priests at her funeral testified to the great esteem in which she was held by them. The Bishop was a personal and intimate friend of Sisters for many years. He visited her regularly every week during her long illness. Many a story he told of his acquaintance with her since boyhood days. He sang the Solemn Requiem Mass and officiated at the graveside. From Heaven Sister will no doubt continue to help by her intercession her dear boys of St. Vincent's. May she rest in peace.

Sister made no great stir during her life, and only briefly after her death. I don't know what science makes of incorruptibility these days or even if it has any significance at all. Maybe it was a sign of Divine approval of the Life of Reilly to her sisters in Community, or maybe it was just a sign of Divine approval of that first House of the Sisters in Ireland, just as the Story of Sister Agnes Hunt in 1886 was taken as a sign of St. Louise's blessing on the new Provincial Seminary in Mill Hill. God knows!

The other members of this family of six were two boys - James and John, one of whom became a priest in America, and two girls, Lizzie and a Mrs. Brannigan.

Perhaps, as might befit a saintly woman, with a "free and unconstrained spirit", another letter appeared from somewhere as I was finalizing this book. It was written to my father on January 20th, 1943, from Scarborough in Yorkshire.

My dear John,

Thank you for your very welcome letter and the lovely snaps of your two fine boys, and your dear little wife, who looks a real mother. How did you get around "the Censor" not to open your letter. If we only send a Holy Picture to Ireland, we get it back by the next post, with yards of instructions! You must have sent the children's Angel Guardian to deliver your letter. How are all your dear ones?…it makes me feel very old, but sure I am 70, and D.V. next year, will be 50 years a Sister. "No chicken" says you. How is James? I knew him better than any of you. He came to see me when he brought cattle over to Scotland years ago, and your noble self I met on my last visit to Drogheda, driving your father R.I.P. to the town.

I expect I will see my dear Ireland from above. I can't expect to live much longer, please pray for me, when you hear I am gone. I hear from "May" (Sr. Anthony) pretty often...We have had our share of Hitler. Our lovely home in Hull is full of soldiers. I am glad the poor lads got a comfortable billet, God help them, they are all torn from their homes, like ourselves.

Kindly remember me to Mary, James and all...and please excuse this scribble, as we used to say long ago, the "Sod of Turf" and penny a week was lost on me.

Bless you all,

Your fond cousin in J.C.,

Sister Mary.

Chapter Five
The Boss

Patrick McCullen was an only son; his mother, Ann Taaffe, had died ten days after his birth, which came on December 21st, 1852. He was reared in Beamore with a household consisting of his father, James, a single aunt, named Jane, who kept house, and another aunt, Mary, her husband Patrick Sheridan and their two daughters, Mary Anne and Bridget. James was a skilled and very successful builder and had also amassed about 150 acres of land and a shareholding in the Drogheda Steampacket Company. Pat was a voracious reader, and his books range from Latin to mathematics and geography to politics, but most particularly history. His name appears among the "Victorian graffiti" on the wall of the inner tomb in Newgrange (orthostat C5), done about 1865, and he was roped in to gather the sticks of the mob in 1868, after the riots in Drogheda, which took place just before the parliamentary election of Benjamin Whitworth.

A story has come down to us via Joe McCullen of Hartlands, that the Boss was earmarked for the life of a builder by his father. He was sent with a horse and cart, and a load of window frames to a building site at Boylans of Hilltown. Whether the frames were badly loaded, or the ropes were not tied, the load fell off on the Beamore Road and the frames were broken. The aftermath of this calamity decided Pat that he preferred the life of a farmer. A man of enormous energy and singlemindedness, he built up his farm by additional leasing and purchasing, and trading in various livestock, including a load of white donkeys assembled for the British Army. A friend of his, Tom McQuillan of Duleek Street, used to say to Pat – "You'll never be happy until you are chained in a goldmine." Another of this McQuillan family who came from Duke Street to Duleek Gate, and would be ancestors of the Burkes from that area, wrote some advice for Pat McCullen in 1877.

Well, do you want my opinion of female beauty, fit for a wife? After a big purse is a hardy, square woman well put on sound legs, a good coarse fiery red head that you could almost see in the dark, strong round arms, red and healthy, that would remind you she could hang a big pot of praties over the fire and lift them off again without taking a feather out of her and that she could churn butter better than a machine. A little wholesome sweat coming through the skin, that tould you she was was moist and healthy, a sizeable bosom, that would put the trembles into a feeding bottle manufacturer. Eyes that can see straight, a nose with a small cock in it, a fair stretch of mouth, and not a little mousehole of a thing as some women have. Sound yellow teeth, that would tear a raspin from a tough crubeen, a short neck, hands and feet to match the body, and then you have a woman that you might call a beauty. Because in such a woman as I have described, you have two things joined together, you have beauty and use. You don't see in that woman a bit of a doll that you could blow off your hand, and would beggar a bank paying doctors for her and poultices and salts and senna.

Whether Pat took the advice or not is open to debate, I am not sure that Annie would have wished to be described in such terms. He was a man who valued thrift, and sought to educate his children in such values.

There is also a story of a small boy sent back into Drogheda to get the proper change, because he came home with a farthing (1/4 d.) less than was due. One of the local rhymes used to go –

> "Pat the Boar,
> Let a roar,
> And frightened all the crows
> In Beamore!"

Almost thirty years after Pat died, my father used to still refer to him as "The Boss". Some of this strong individualism can be caught from the pre-wedding photograph of himself and his best man, Nicholas Moran of Julianstown, in 1881. Having observed my father's thrift, determination / stubbornness and high principle, I can only imagine similar characteristics in "The Boss".

Pat McCullen (Groom) seated, and Nicholas Moran of Julianstown (Bestman) standing, before the wedding in February 1881

His Letters to Annie

Thirteen of these survive and they give some idea of the travelling in search of gold, the dictatorial style, and the reliance on the manageress at home. Unfortunately, he was a man in a hurry, so no dates appear on the letters…

Dublin, Sunday

Dearest,

    Should the slater require a small ladder or two, send to Mr. Porters (Beabeg) for the lend of them. Caution him to examine them and the ropes before he uses them as I won't be accountable.

    Your,

    Pat.

No address

Dearest,

    I have heard that Mrs. Rooney, Hilltown, is dead. James might go a short distance with funeral should he find it convenient. He can enquire time.

    Pat.

Clones,
Thursday 1.30p.m.

Dearest,

    A very fine day here, no rain last night. James should see if ground is dry enough to put out manure in Rabbitys — if so, let him stay himself and lead the carts and keep the horses working well. Should any sheep remain to be shorn, let them be done.

    Your,

    P. McCullen.

Headford,
Saturday, 3 o'clock.

Annie,

    Just arrived here, quite well and fresh from Kenmare with six cows, 20 Irish miles, stopped at a village, Kilgarvan, about midway, last night with a friend of Johnny Langan's, Battramstown. The road from Headford to Kenmare runs through a valley about 40 perches wide the whole way from which the mountains arise quite straight. I go to Killorglin tonight, as there is no train from Killarney tomorrow. Tuesday morning next, D.V., let Jemmy Gallagher leave on 20 minutes to 10 train and come to Hazelhatch by train leaving Kingsbridge about noon. He will get the cattle from the stationmaster there. Kisses for you all including Mother and Joe [This must have been written about 1892.] I hope Paddy won't eat too much eggs tomorrow. Let McDermot get the cow. No more now <u>dearest</u> from your Pat.

Oldcatle,

Sunday.

Annie,

    I hope you and Bab are quite well. There was no cows in Granard, got four in Edgeworthstown will go to Ballyduff tomorrow. You will want to send to Peter Dowdall, the Clerk of the Union, immediately on receipt of this for a licence to take 20 cattle from Oldcastle into Drogheda and when it is got let it be given to Hamill, the driver of the 10 o'clock train, who will take it over to the stationmaster here. Perhaps your Uncle John or Mangan would be able to give it. Let there be no more time lost. If the 10 o'clock train is missed, send it by six in the evening as I cannot leave here without it.

    Yours,

    Patrick McCullen.

No address (Dublin?)

Dearest,

    Butter a very small market. Got a firkin from Byrne. I could not get a cool, so I had to fall back on Danish. Byrne had none of it in the store but expected by this evening's boat, so it may not arrive with the firkin – you can have enquiries made at Railway. The Lucan Dairy will send a can of milk. I have been to Gerrard's office. What he wants is probate of R. Pentony's will (I expect Johnny has it). He also wants deed of release signed by you and May. If Cissie has such tell her to send it at once, as these are the only things wanted to have sale complete.

    Your,

    Pat.

I could get a letter at Balla Post Office or Athlone.

Balla,

Sunday evening.

Dearest

    There was a very heavy fall of snow here. If there was the same with you, the cattle in Mathews' field will want hay. Tell James not to let them be neglected. You might also have inquiry made at the Railway if the grains did not come. Have the clay taken from the sides of the grain pit in the garden. The barn will hold the Dublin grains.

    Your,

    Pat.

Claremorris,
Monday, 9 p.m.

Dear Annie,

I trust you are all well. I bought 30 cattle in Balla today. Send Curran to Hill of Down, and send brand. I was in Ballinrobe. Mary Anne was received today. They both seem very well and happy. I will go to Athlone tonight, and can't say when I will be home. Do the best you can till then.

Your,

Pat.

Note: The reception mentioned is that of his cousin and family member, Mary Anne Sheridan, who with her sister, Bridget, both entered the Mercy Order in Ballinrobe.

Belfast,
Wednesday morning.

Dearest Annie,

I intend to go on to Dublin direct. In case I buy any lambs tomorrow I will send a telegram to Tom Woods. Send Gallagher out to him same as last time, before the 10 o'clock train, and tell him to go to Ganly's Stand – *if he gets word.*

Kisses for you all from,

Your,

Pat.

Undated & no address

Dearest Annie,

I hope the weather is fine and that you have them drawing the hay. When ready, draw Road field and make it into Pike or rick down haggard. *Don't* put any where rick was last year at piggery. Kisses for all, and a dozen for Annie,

From,

Pat.

Roscommon Town.

Dearest,

Here I am in the best of form, T.G., after driving over from Strokestown. I will have to remain here tonight to go to Balla by train tomorrow. I bought 20 cattle today. They average £10 each. I think them dearer than last year. Let James do his best to mind everything until I get home. He should see to the cattle in Mathews' field.

Your,

Pat.

Mullingar,
Friday evening.

Dearest,

I am sorry to see James Moran's death in today's paper. I hope you sent James to he funeral. The last two days have been very fine. I hope progress has been made with the mangold. If the ground is fit tomorrow the remaining ground might be got ready and drills opened. You might get some salt. I think Mrs. Stokes is cheapest. Let James make a bargain with her one and a half tons will be wanted. Spread all the dung possible and have the drills closed. Nicholas Connor can sow the salt. I have been out at Gaybrook but did not see the Colonel – he was fishing. Bought 10 cattle in Athlone, only one cow. Seen James Reilly – his hand has been very sore but is now almost well. I go down to Roscommon tonight. No more now from your

Pat.

Cunninghams Comm. Hotel,
Ballinrobe.
Wednesday evening, 189-

Dearest,

James tells me there is a sore on the chestnut horse's back – if so don't send him to Dublin on Friday. Send the black in his stead, and should there be any sores on his back or shoulders, don't send him, but let Nicholas go with one only, the mare.

<u>On no account let a horse with a sore go to Dublin.</u> I bought 42 cattle today. Trusting you and all are well.

Your, Pat.

Pat and Annie

The Domestic Scene

As you may recall, James was born in December 1881. Judging by the letters and commands from the Boss, he got more than his share of responsibility and sometimes reacted. Annie acted as the go-between, the diplomat and the peacemaker. Life between marriage in 1881 and 1900 must have been hectic. They had eight children, as follows:

James Joseph	Tuesday 20.12.81
Mary Frances	Friday 28.9.83
Richard Joseph	Sunday 17.5.85
Patrick Dominic	4.8.87
John Alphonsus	25.9.89
Joseph	1.9.91
Henry Vincent (Hal)	Sunday 21.1.94
Anthony Joseph	Friday 21.1.98

In that same two decades, Pat's father James died in 1877, aged 60 years. Annie's Aunt Maggie and her daughter Margaret, aged 19 years, died in 1878 and her mother, Mary, died in 1898. Mary Moore entered an convent in Hereford in March 1896. The Espousal Window in St. Mary's Church, Drogheda, is a memorial to Maggie and her daughter.

Pat did not get on at all well with his uncle-in-law, Patrick Sheridan, and when Aunt Mary died on 31.12.1883, Mr. Sheridan moved out, and the two Miss Sheridans later entered the Mercy Order. Due to pressure of space, the house was extended around 1890, a large haybarn was erected in 1896, and an extra range of cowsheds, a loft, and a piggery were all constructed. Extra lands were being purchased or leased, and it is easy to understand why Annie would not have much letter writing time…

Her second last son, Hal, was mentally handicapped, and there were nine men working on the farm. The wagebook shows the names and amounts paid to each for a six-day week in July 1901…

	Pay per week
James Connor	12 shillings
Nicholas Connor	12 shillings
Patrick Faulkner	12 shillings
Henry Malin	12 shillings
Christopher Reilly	12 shillings
Dominick Lynch	12 shillings
Patrick Kelly	9 shillings
John Monaghan	8 shillings 9 pence
James Melia	12 shillings

In addition, Pat was heavily involved in business ventures outside the farm and as a political supporter of land reform. Evidence of this is found in the £5 payment to Charles S. Parnell in 1881, his opposition to the Board of the Drogheda Steampacket Company in 1898 the foundation of the Louth-Meath Dead Meat Society in 1904 and shareholding (30) in the Dogheda Waterworks Company, purchased in 1892.

Annie was an integral part of all these ventures and examples survive of letters written by Pat, corrected for grammar and flow by her, and then finished for dispatch by Pat. The new farms at Salmon, Balbriggan (1903), and Diamor, Kells (1893), were purchased and a new dwelling house constructed at Salmon. This latter holding was bought in Annie's own name and later became home to James. The level of debate within the family must have been very wide and when Pat became one of the liquidators of the Steampacket Company in 1901, it was he who originated a scheme to minimize tax payments on the deposit interest. The form of payment was modelled on one used by the Bahia and San Francisco Railway Company. A special Bill to liquidate the Steampacket Company was brought in the British Parliament, in 1902, sponsored by Sir William Hornby, Mr. Fielden, Mr. T.M. Healy, and Mr. Joseph Nolan.

At this stage it is fitting to move from the large stage of Westminster, and the Land Acts, which made tenant farmers secure and more progressive, to the very important world of the two eldest children, James and Mary, both of whom were starting to write letters of their own to Annie…

House and outbuildings (circa 1960) at Beamore

Chapter Six

James – The Unwilling Scholar

James McCullen,
pictured at St. Finian's Seminary, Navan, June 1896

In the "Annals of St. Mary's School", the rollbook of 1892 lists James McCullen from Beamore and son of a "farmer", aged 11 years, "never at school before". This is not unusual, as the age of entry to the school varies widely from five up to fourteen. The majority would have been aged seven or eight. It is surprising considering the value put on education in the family, and the fact that three members of the Beabeg McCullens had all started in the school in previous years, aged from six upwards. References to nuns in James' own letters suggest that he was at the Mercy Convent school for some years before transferring to St. Mary's B.N.S. at the age of eleven.

In later years, James, who was a very colourful personality, would regale myself and my brother with stories of life at "Mickey McLoughlin's" Academy, where he used to go with his lunch in his top pocket, and flavour the sandwiches during the day, with the spits of chewed tobacco. He even demonstrated the angle of spit necessary to hit the bread! James was a master of delivery and would make the most outrageous jokes while keeping a totally straight face. Two letters of his to Mary and Richard, his sister and brother, aged 12 and 10, survive…

Both are written from the Seminary, Navan, and dated October 19th, 1895.

Dear Mary

…I wish you success in your music. I am sure you will do something in it. It will not be long until Xmas vacation. It is nine weeks today. I hope you will not have your party until then. I am as ever, your fond brother,

James.

Note: Mary's party was due on September 28th !

Dear Richard,

I hope you are getting on well at Geography and that you are still great with Mother Catherine. Which was it, you or Paddy, who sent down the nice apple? Whichever of you it was, I am very thankful for it. I hope the football has not yet met with an untimely end. I am, as ever,

Your fond brother, James.

There may have been too many distractions at home or perhaps James was being groomed for some career other than farming, but whatever the reason, he commenced boarding in the Seminary, then situated in Navan, in Autumn of 1894, at the age of almost thirteen. He spent two years of imprisonment in that establishment, which is colourfully described by Richard, in a recording done with Father Gerry Rice in the 1970s; Richard, afterwards a Monsignor and sometime President of the College when he moved to Mullingar, describes pupils wrapped in rugs to keep warm at classtime, and sticking slabs of butter on the underside of the table to save some for tea, not to mention the meat, which was green in colour! Plain speaking seems to have been a family trait.

There survives twenty-eight letters from James, all but two are sent to his Mother, and the two are addressed to Father. Some are dated, but many just have the day of the week.

Saturday (undated)
Probably 1894

My dear Mother,

I received yours on Thursday, and I am sorry I could not answer it before this, but the trunks cannot be opened unless on Saturday. I could not get any notepaper out before this. I am quite well and happy, though lonesome sometimes. I have been put into French, Algebra, Euclid, Arithmetic and English classes. I do think I will be learning Latin or Greek. If you have any of the books, you might send them on at once, as I can do very little without them. I want a Primary English Grammar by Hall, price 8d. immediately and I think I might get them here. It is carpet bags, boys here generally use for sending home washing. I would be very thankful to you if you would send me two of them. I was agreeably surprised when unpacking my trunk I got a present of a lovely set of beads – thank her on my behalf. Tell John I will pay my dues at Xmas. If you please send scissors and clothes brush. I forgot to put a lock on my case when coming.

We went out to walk as far as Kilcarne on Wenesday. There are almost seventy boys here and a good many from about Oldcastle. I suppose Father is very busy now with the threshing. I hope he is quite well and shall be expecting some of you down, very soon, let me know when you can come down. If Mary and Richard are going to write, let them enclose it in yours. I suppose the whole of you, and Aunts are quite well – please write soon as possible. I am as ever,

Your fond son, James.

Saturday (undated)

Private — not for small boys eyes.

My dear Mother,

I wrote you on last Tuesday, and I was uneasy during the week at not having received an answer, however you can tell me that in your next letter. Tell Father the Euclid is safe and that I shall send it home in my bag...We commenced work on Wednesday and all the boys are back now. Who is the prospective member for Louth? I hope the Meath ex-member will be successful. The weather is all that could be desired here. Do not forget to send stamps — I hope to receive a letter from Joseph soon.

(Joe would have been three years old.)

Saturday (undated)

...You need not send any sheets or pillow cases next time...I also received newspaper cuttings enclosed in your letter...I have a chance of going home as I do not live far. I forgot ever to enquire for the new Steamer. I suppose she is over by this anyway. I hope Joe is better...I suppose John is paddling through the wet as ever. We have snow and frost here. I suppose the nuns are busy selling tickets for the raffle and that Mary is having her revenge on Richard by selling as much as possible and gaining as much importance...I am afraid I will have to spend the day of the raffle here...

Tuesday (undated)

...If you intend sending jam in the next bag you might send an old spoon as it would greatly facilitate matters. I am sorry that Margaret did not see me but tell her I am very thankful...I have heard of Master Fox of Oldcastle, he is an only son. ..they mad a mistake when they put an "a" instead of an "e" in McCullen...please find out T. Symington's address...do not forget studs...I am quite well...Richard will have to learn dancing...did not receive Joseph's letter yet, when it comes, I trust it will be "lyting" and not "scribbles". I hope Father will be down on Saturday. Tell Aunts to write soon...

Monday (undated)

I received bag all right on Saturday evening. ..You may expect me home on the train leaving here at 9.10 and reaching Drogheda at 9.35 on Monday morning. There has been no official announcement as yet but I will not write again...home on Monday morning. As I will see you all soon, I will not say much.

Tuesday night

It was officially announced that we will get home on Saturday morning…do not forget to send Postal Order in time…The girls in the convent are getting home tomorrow, and that is the reason we are getting home before Monday. Needless to say, I am quite well…I was remarked the other day for being so fat, as you will soon have an opportunity to prove. I hope you let John and Joe to the raffle today and that they paid a visit to the refreshment stall…

14-3-1895

I was disappointed at not getting a letter from you this week but I have my doubts that the last letter I gave in on Saturday last was posted. Fr. Curry was down here yesterday – he looks older and fatter than ever I saw him before. Is there any truth in the rumour that he was going away? He talked as if he were, for when one of the ___ asked him if it were true, he seemed to evade it by asking "What made you think of that?" (Of course, you need not say anything about it.)

The incoming letters were not opened – I think it was only a threat. What is going on in the garden at the moment? Peas should be down by this. Is there any news about? What is Oweney Whearthy at now? I did not get a letter from Aunts and hope they are all well…no more news…I hope that Owen alias Boney alias Michael Reilly and Bridget (Lynch), have signed a truce…

12-10-1895

…they ought to be drawing in the hay now. I hope the Beabegs people are quite well. You might tell me if Charlie Reilly is gone back to Dundalk and if T. Symington is at home at present. We will have two examinations before vacation. Father Crean was up here last Thursday…There will be a great feast of apples and other things which will cost two and sixpence. I have got an arithmetic here second-hand for sixpence…I hope it will not be long until I have the pleasure of seeing you…I got the overcoat all right…I did not receive a letter from Mother Catherine or my Aunts yet…

19-10-1895

…I was thinking of seeing Father. It might be better begin Latin or Greek now but will have additional subjects after Xmas, but as you and Father are the best judges I will do nothing until I either hear from you or see one of you. I would be glad if you could send me a pair of gloves (woolen will do) as my hands be very cold in the mornings. Is Lizzie Reilly still stopping with my Aunts? Did Mrs. Conner recover the *turkey or is she going to get its' value off the County?* [Maggie Connor, and the survival or demise of her poultry, were a cause celebre in the locality, and she went to court to seek damages against Mrs. McEvoy's dog in 1904.] *Which of the Miss Moores got married? Were you not at the wedding? I seen Father Crean today – he is looking quite well and was after riding from Drogheda to Oldcastle. You will, I hope, come down soon, and not let it be like your visit to Dalkey. I suppose you know we have a new Professor...I hope Paddy's pigs are getting fat...*

9-11-1895

(This is a serious business letter to Father)

My dear Father,

I commenced Latin and Greek yesterday and I think I ought to get on fairly well at it. I gave my Mother a list of books which I will require...I will send my bag on this day week, if you are not down before then. We had examinations here this week which lasted two days. Will you please tell me in answering this how many cattle have you tied in this year and if you opened any of the grain pits yet. I hope to be home with you on this day six weeks so that we will not feel the passing of time. I hope all are quite well – Mother told me Mrs, Healy died. Have the Contractors for Milk and Butter in Drogheda Union given satisfaction lately? They used to give much trouble. I suppose the Corporation did not buy the Waterworks – I hope to receive a letter from you soon...

Note: The Drogheda Union contracts were being supplied by Pat McCullen...

15-11-1895

I was disappointed at not receiving an answer from my father but I suppose he was too busy to write. I wrote also to Mother Catherine and Aunt Cissie with the same result, however, I hope you will be more diligent in answering this letter. My name was taken down in the Intermediate list for the Junior Grade. I had a visit early in the week from Father Curry – he says you are all quite well. Please let me know if my father has got any of the books yet. I have got Tom Symington's address and shall write to him soon. I would be glad if you could tell me when I may hope for a visit from Father. I hope all are well especially Mary.
P.S. You might send in my bag next time an old Drogheda Newspaper.

J.McC.

20-11-1895

...I heard Bob Symington is an uncle again. I hope he does not feel indignant at being so titled...Tell (or send a dispatch, or have an item inserted in the Beamore Advertiser) Miss M. Catherine that I will answer her note personally, as none of you can expect to hear much news from me here, unless I

manufacture it…no news here at all…send me an epitome of it in your letters…I am quite well as it is difficult to be otherwise when one has nothing to do (manually). I am fairly contented at the prospect of vacation…

Saturday (undated)

…I hope Father will come down on Monday…I suppose Mary is very far advanced in her music. Richard ought to be very learned in Geography now. I hope Paddy is making satisfactory progress…I hope there is not much blood spilled between Mickey Connor and Owen particularly as they are at the stallfeeding.. .Tell Richard to inform Bridget Cunningham to keep some apples for me if possible…Needless to ask for John or Joe – I hope the latter will not be too lonesome for John after Xmas when he goes to school…There is a play being prepared here called "The Youthful Martyrs of Rome" – the same as Fabiola which is in Father Crean's library…As I have exhausted my tongue, I will now conclude.

December 14th, 1895

…disappointed at no letter from Duleek Gate…forgot to wish you Happy Birthday…will write to warn you when we are to be let loose…great night here on the 12th – St. Finian's Day – when we got as many cakes as we could devour. The Bishop and a good deal of priests were in …have compassion on me and send me my passage, if my father cannot be down, send a postal order, blank, and the Dean will change it…and don't forget a stamp or two.

25-1-1896

…disappointed at no visit from Father…I am prepared against disappointment now as it is so uncertain what time he drops in…I managed to hear last night about Fr. Doyle – did he have full use of his faculties when he was dying?…The Intermediate will commence on the 10th of June and will occupy a week – then four days of retreat…We shall get home on 26th June 1896 A.D.

Without giving you false hopes, or myself, rather, I think there is some prospect of me getting home at Easter…some of the boys from Oldcastle got home last year. However, it will be only for the day…

I would not like to have to remain here more than a year and I am glad I will not have to come back after Summer. I was very thankful for the presents I got, and hope they shall not be levied off me for Paddy's birthday. We are all well here, and the cane in full swing once more – I hope the Beabegs are quite well, I think I shall write to Henry soon.

February 9th, 1896

I require my Certificate of Birth…for the Intermediate Examinations…Baptismal Cert. Will not do, but this must be got from the Clerk of the Union at a cost of 3s and 7d. I suppose Joseph is keeping correction over the whole of you…

Saturday (undated)

I received the note and Certificate...I had Aunt May down here on Thursday and Father Curry this morning, so that I was not badly off for visitors...

Saturday, February 1896

...received your letter including scraps (one of them a bit too personal about getting up in the morning). I hope you enjoyed the fifteenth anniversary of your wedding...I hope you will let Paddy, Richard and John stay at home for the mill. As I have lent Richard the strap I will let Paddy hold onto the top, in trust.

I think I am getting on fairly well at my studies, anyway, I am not wasting any time, but doing my best. Was there any person nominated for South Louth. Is there any chance for Fullam? I seen in a piece of a newspaper a report of a meeting of Louth and Meath Farmers – I did not see my father but noticed several bloodthirsty patriots were there...

February 22ⁿᵈ.

...I suppose you were too busy. I hope Joseph ate a fair share of pancakes and that he goes to see the jam pretty often, with a spoon, of course. I need not ask about Paddy's appetite – I hope John did good work too.

Is Tom Mooney's dog getting anything to do, or are there any lambs yet? I saw some a month ago, and they were pretty big – I hope you have a fair supply of jam for the garrison – don't let supplies run down for my sake, as there is plenty of jam going here...

Friday night.

My dearest Mother,

I received your letter this morning and I am sorry that anything I wrote in my last letter might have given offence to you but no matter how long I shall remain here it shall not make me change my mind a bit as to what I intend to be and which I told you about last Summer. I am sorry I forgot to send home a piece of cake to Joseph...I shall follow your advice about writing to Beabeg. Did you commence gardening operations yet? I hope you will find volunteer gardeners. I hope John is progressing at the tablets and Richard at dancing...I sympathise with Paddy at the Owen Roes defeat and that they got an opportunity of presenting themselves with leathern medals.

Saturday, April 25th.

...*I hear that the appointment for which Fr. Curry was mentioned was filled up. However I cannot say much for its truth...(Here follows two sentences in French!) The excursion this year will I hear be to Clogher Head but there is no chance of me getting home for the day...I will be at home this day nine weeks anyway, and I hope it will be for good.*

I think I knew the boy that was drowned in the Nanny...I did not know you had to go to the dentist...I hope you will let Joseph walk in the next procession...There was what was considered unfair play at the Concert last week I, giving the performers extra cakes which ended in a stone being pegged in the window and nearly breaking a silver jug. Expulsion, etc., was threatened but as the culprit could not be found, nothing came of it.

As ever,

Your fond son, James.

Monday (undated)

...*We got leave to wear straw hats, I would be glad if you could put one in my bag, size 7 will fit me...I am going in for English, Euclid, French, Arithmetic and Algebra. I am giving up Latin and Greek....I can then give more time to other subjects. We all returned well from Gormanstown...the boys enjoyed themselves...to hear some of them talk of Drogheda Station, you would think they were comparing it to Euston in London. Others never saw the sea before and several mistook Aunt Cissie for my sister. This, you may tell her, is a very high compliment to pay her...you might also send me a pair of studs in the bag.*

Late Spring, 1896

...*I got the hat (no. 2) all right – it was much admired...I was very glad to get a letter from Aunt May. She said, "People thought she had wonderful courage to leave country but that she would scarcely have courage enough to come back now.". I hope that nothing serious happened to Richard. The hieroglyphics at the end of the letter was meant for an answer about putting something extra in the bag...*

What sort of vegetables are the gardeners sowing at present – they must be either too early or <u>too late.</u> I am sure Paddy is very proud of the rowing club colours...John, I am sure is dividing his time between study and <u>work</u> – he is, I think, not the worst of your gardeners. I hope Mary is getting better...

23-5-1896

...*I also got the hat safely, I like it very well and it is just my fit. By the way, a boy from Mullingar asked me to get a hat for him, so I ask Mary to get one from Brady's...We were over at the Convent Baths at Athlumney last week. There are two baths, a cold and a warm one...Who is Red Reilly No. 2? Where did Philip disappear to or where is Jamie Gallagher now? Was Paddy at the Drogheda Fair (12ᵗʰ May). I am sure Joseph is keeping correction on the whole lot of you, Hal will soon be his aide-de-camp. I am sorry to hear of the death of Richard's pinkeens. I hope himself and John will catch some more…*

June 6ᵗʰ.

My dear Father

…Class broke up here today, so that we will have a week's revision (vulgarly called "pounding"). I am sorry to hear that Mattie Kelly is so bad. The boats on the canal caused great commotion here- some of the day boys were picturing themselves going across at least to England - I heard that one of the boats got stuck somewhere about Slane and they had to throw some of the cargo overboard. Three at the most is all that will pass out of our class in Junior Grade…I have as good a chance as any…As we never see anything in the way of haymaking, I do not know what is going on. Richard must have difficulty in cooling the milk in this hot weather…Mr. O'Connell is reported to be getting worried… The potatoes are coming up very well and beginning to blossom…

Monday (undated)

Presumably June '96

My dear Mother

We will get home on the train on Saturday morning…I have not so bad a chance as I thought in Arithmetic…I have three sums right…The retreat will finish on Friday night, so the train which I will be on, will arrive at 9.25…

As ever, your fond son,

James

True to his word James did not return to the seminary, and became a farmer at the age of fifteen, which must have been a considerable help to his mother, although she continued to act as the mediatrix between himself and the Boss, and this took some energy and skill. The farm at Salmon, Balbriggan, purchased in Annie's name eventually became James' home and his farming continued for sixty years. He married Annie Grimes in October 1923.

He also acted as a cattle and sheep market reporter for local newspapers for many years, using the keen observational skills and quick turn of phrase developed in his schooldays.

Great emphasis was placed on academic achievements amongst the family and all kinds of certificates were framed and hung on the walls. Some examples are Mary's London College of Music Certificate and the Souvenir of First Holy Communion and Confirmation of Richard. It is interesting to note that he received his First Communion at the age of ten, but was confirmed at nine, the previous year. James seems to have sacrificed such glory for the world of fresh air and livestock markets, without too much grief.

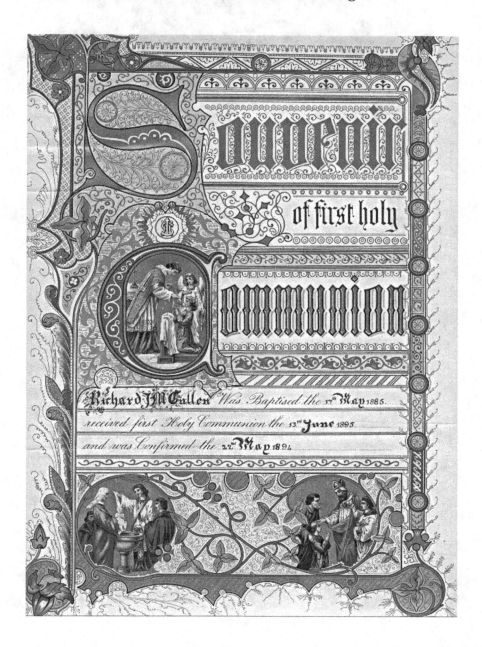

Chapter Seven
Letters from the Convent

Sister Anthony of Padua Moore

In the 1890s, Annie had three surviving sisters living in the Pub at Duleek Gate. They were Mary Jane, known as "Sissy", Teresa and Mary, known as "May". In 1896, May decided to enter an convent at Bartestree, in Hereford. You may recall how her nephew James described her as "very brave" to leave her country and join the daughters of Our Lady of Charity, at the age of thirty years. Her name in religion became Sister Anthony of Padua Moore, and for sixty years she continued to write to her sisters, nephews, nieces, grandnephews and grandnieces, and to send needlework presents, pin-cushions, scapulars and Agnus Dei, and baby clothes and pyjama cases of all kinds.

There is a fascinating book put together by the Nuns for the Diamond Jubilee of Sister Anthony in 1959, where they imitated the Eamon Andrews format of "This is your Life" and brought on various guests to regale the Community with their experiences of Sister, as a Mistress of Novices, Infirmarian, Portress, Robriere, Superior, Sister Assistant and Directress of the Laundry. The surprise guests included many Nuns, Saint Patrick himself, Pope John XXIII, her grandniece Sister Magdalen McCullen D.C., and her grandnephew Rev. Father Richard McCullen. The book includes her Golden Jubilee Programme from 1949, which was a performance of "Cinderella".

At the time of the Diamond Jubilee celebrations, Sister Anthony was aged 93 years, and had long out-lived all the members of her family. Her presence still pervades the archives in Beamore, sometimes an embroidered pin-cushion or a delicate lace prayer, and surprisingly, I found an unusual keepsake of Annie's in the iron-clad safe in the house. Wrapped in cellophane paper and carefully placed at the back of the various documents was a length of auburn hair, sent home from the convent at Bartestree in 1896, plaited for all its eighteen inches.

There is a small bundle of sixteen letters written to her big Sister, Annie, who was almost twelve years older than May. Before considering these, there is one surviving letter from Sissy, written to Annie in 1877, when she was just sixteen and Annie was twenty-two.

St. Mary's Convent Schools,
Drogheda.
February 7th, 1877

My dearest Annie,

I suppose you will be delighted to receive this little note from me as it is so long since I wrote to you. I am drawing a very nice lady's head. I expect to have it finished before Easter. I am learning a very difficult piece I think I won't have it off till the Summer Examinations. The weather is getting so fine now we get out every day at recreation. It was a great pity that the building of the new Convent was stopped, but the weather is so fine now, I suppose they will begin again. I will have to be getting up early next week to go to mass. I think it is to nine I will go. Teresa and May unite with me in fond love to you, Mamma and Father. As ever, dearest Annie,

Your affectionate sister,

Sissy,

Enfant de Marie.

Considering that they lived in the same house as each other, and that St. Mary's was not a boarding school, this was obviously an exercise which the Nuns encouraged during school-time.

From our Monastery of Bartestree, Hereford
April (1896?)

My dear Annie,

I was delighted to receive your Easter card. I suppose you had James home for Easter, and I hope he is not changing his mind. I will be so glad when he comes to visit here, and you can tell John there are lots of schools near here whenever he likes to come, dear Annie, the country here is delightful – I suppose you got a full account of the beautiful Convent, also of the Rev. Mother, as Pat had the pleasure of meeting her. I have met a sister here who appreciates Father O'R. S.J. as much as you do!...

Tell Mary the Sisters here wear white. I am sure she would like it –

Kindest remembrance – I am dear Annie

Your fond sister,

May. P.S. I will expect a letter.

May 11ᵗʰ, 1896

My dear own Annie,

I know it is a disgrace not having written to you before — you may be last but not least. Now, I was so glad to receive your letter but you are as stiff as ever and would not let me have another until I write — is that it?

I do feel how thoughtless I may have been in so many ways. Sweet Mother Mine. Thanks awfully for the Missal, it is nice. I hope you will succeed in getting the photo from Father Curry.

You had James very near home — it is well he did not <u>bolt</u> but then he is not like his Aunt, he is more like his Godmother — our gentle lamb. She is good. It is well for people who do not have to keep trying to be gentle, like you. I am so glad Mary was successful with her music — that was a good number of marks and will encourage her. Tell Richard I hope Charly is as well as ever — perhaps I may write to Navan next week, but then I do not like such critics as they may meet with there — they would be almost as bad as the <u>Drogheda critics</u>. You should get Cis to enquire from Nelly Macken of Clonswords about Bellingham School. Her sister is a nun there and Dr. Adrian's children are there, it is not far from Hereford. Mary might like it and then I would see some of you.

Tell Cis the Founder of this Order is Ven. John Eudes. Teresa is studying a very interesting book. Tell her I may require other things more when she disposes of some of our stock. Did she sell the pet lamb yet? I would have a claim on that. Bear and lamb always disagree.

Cissy wants to know why I say I am so happy, well, I will not define it exactly now. Tell her I always did like novelty. We had one today, such a group of clergy — quite a number, beginning with our Director, Fr. Lewis. If on Earth, there is a happy state, it is the religious state…

Your loving God-daughter and sister,

Postulant of Our Lady of Charity.

May 23ʳᵈ, 1896

I am sure "Sweet Marie" as I need to call her did not approve of Bellingham, nor would I, so I hope to see you by some other means…Our Mother Superior has been re-elected. I would like to write more about the Community, which I hope you will see someday. Our Sr. Mary of St. Celia has made up the leaves so nicely for Hal. I hope he is getting strong. He had Fr. Curry's blessing before the Oblates'…

The Prayer for Ireland, for Marie (M.F.)

"May it again become the seat of learning and religion. May the rising generation see its rights restored."

…What would you say to the Dominican Convent, Galway, for Mary? She would get accustomed to the white habit…

Your loving Sister Moore,

Postulant of Our Lady of Charity.

December 21ˢᵗ, 1896

My dearest Annie,

…I was trying to think what age James will be this month, he must be quite a young man. Cissie will have no excuse if she wants someone to take her over to see me. Will Marie ever forgive me not writing to her but then she knows how quick the time goes in a convent – is that one of her objections to them? I believe she is not very partial. I am afraid she will agree with her Aunt Cissie…

…quite a time of trouble to Fr. Curry…some of the trials God sends to "try His own" as He chastise those that He loved. That is one thing Dr. Hedley tried to make us remember…

January 29ᵗʰ, 1898

My own dear Annie,

I must congratulate you on the arrival of the seventh son…it was not such a surprise as I had a guess from your letter and was very anxious to hear from some of you…I wonder you did not coax Mary to write to me during vacation…how will she ever reconcile herself to all those dear, troublesome, brothers?

Give my love to that young namesake of mine, perhaps he will have the kindness to write to his Aunt, not like other nephews I know…I would not ask him to be so quiet as dear little Hal. You ought to see after him or you may regret it.

I was so glad to receive a letter from Millockstown. I hope Mrs. Reilly's health will improve.

April 19ᵗʰ, 1899

My dear Mary,

…We are preparing for holy Profession. Secure all the prayers you can for us…you will have to make an attempt at singing, when at home with all these brothers, as I expect you will be a model sister. We are expecting Father Curry for the ceremony and of course Father Fitzmaurice…with over two hundred children, we can find something to employ us…

December, 1899

My dear James,

...an answer to your letter of May the 15th, I am ashamed at not answering...your Father gave me an agreeable surprise of a visit...he must think me a matter of fact Nun, to give him such a catechizing...I suppose you have the new byke by this time...all very interested in the War. I am not sorry the English have met their match, it is not Ireland they have got to deal with, but I do feel sorry they are losing so many of their soldiers — it is cruel work for the possession of a country.

April 1900

My dearest Annie,

...sorry to hear you had such a lot of trouble...hope all are now recovered, especially James...thank you for the papers, I must ask you to discontinue sending them as our Dear Honoured Mother does not wish us to have them unless something very interesting...if you should send some cuttings or of course The Messenger, I will be very glad. I was pleased to know the Queen paid a visit to the Emerald Isle. I hope she was well received.

July 28th, 1900

...I was sorry to hear of the death of Aunt Hickey [Note: the third wife of John Moore]. I know how grieved you must be...I hope it will not have a bad affect on Sissy now in her present state of health...very sad to hear of Dora's dying so suddenly...every consolation in knowing Aunt had such spiritual help...

Sorry to know Cissy is suffering from such extreme weakness...must hope for an improvement when this great heat is over...also hope you will have good news of Hal...you must not fret about him. I hope your patience will be rewarded, it is a trouble bringing him to Dublin so often...

December 20th, 1900

I was very pleased to get the photo of John...see how they grow...no one would imagine to look at his placid face he has got such a will of his own. Does he remember when I tried to persuade him he would get a "turnip" if he did not do what I told him. I suppose you know I got one of "Ants" curls from Teresa — he seems a great favourite with them at home...What does Richard intend to do with himself — it is quite time he would make up his mind...So James is crossing to Glasgow — I hope he will take a turn to Bartestree...I hope you correspond with Agnes Reilly. I often think how they get on. I am sure Alice is quite grown — is she as handsome as she promised to be? I wonder if any of them will choose religious life, having so many nuns in the family before...I often think of their Mother, and all her hopes, how they must miss her...you should take a great interest in them. Very sad news Tilly Symington got — I suppose there is no doubt as to the certainty of all lives being lost…it is best to know the truth at once…I hope Hal is growing strong, poor little fellow, does he make an attempt to learn anything?

July 3ʳᵈ, 1901

Thank you for the nice packet of chocolates…Mary…I am glad you are keeping her from school, for your own sake…so much anxiety over Hal…to hear of the death of Patrick Campbell…least expected…sure Mary is inconsolable…I am pleased you are thinking of coming over this year.

July 26ᵗʰ, 1902

….Your visit was so short, I scarcely realised you were here when you left us…I am pleased to know Hal was quite good in your absence…disagreeable not meeting the boat at Liverpool…I hope you will take advantage of all the driving for the rest of the season and mind yourself as I think you require a little care, and get up some more strength…Fr. Fitz. is the "best little Father in the wide, wide world"…

With love, to the Pater and your own dear self…

September 23ʳᵈ, 1902

Congratulations on Richard's success…I hope he took the Exhibition as well…trusting he will be firm learning to bear and forbear…the finer the grinding, the better the flour, as the "Master of Eloquence" used to express it…he has now got an aim in life…I was hoping to hear Hal is improving…special novena by Sr. M. St. Agnes for him.

What have I done to Mary – she never thinks of writing…I am sorry to hear Fr. Curry is suffering so, as sickness takes all our energy…

Our dear Mother very kindly allowed me to have my teeth attended to, so I am happy to say, although I had so many removed, they have not caused any bad effects – it will be some time before they are replaced…thank you for the photo of Joe, I like it very much…

June 3ʳᵈ, 1903

I thought that I had written last…Teresa told me of the death of Maggie Andrews – poor little soul, what a short life, R.I.P.

About Cissy and Teresa's affairs, I was rather surprised – you had never mentioned the subject before. I hope they will soon come to terms. Of course they will have some contention about it for some time, however all will come right, I am sure. I was of your mind about Teresa. I do not quite approve of her keeping the business…

December 19ᵗʰ, 1903

…I suppose James has not yet settled in Scotland, as for Mary, I am sure she forgets she ever had an Aunt May. Teresa told me P.D. is with the Dominican Fathers, I am very glad – does he still think of *the medicine line?…She said Hal is still the same delicate boy…I am sorry there is no improvement…he may be your crown…I send a special love to my little dear Antoine…I am sorry things are not finished up at Beamore Road yet…Teresa has great courage…I hope she will be able to manage…it would seem wiser to have given it up, and taken her portion…I do think you might write oftener…*

> *United by our dear Rev. Mother and dear Sister Assistant,*
>
> *We remain in union with the sacred hearts of Jesus and Mary,*
>
> *Your loving sister,*
>
> *Sr. M. of St. Antoin Moore, Religious of Our Lady of Charity.*

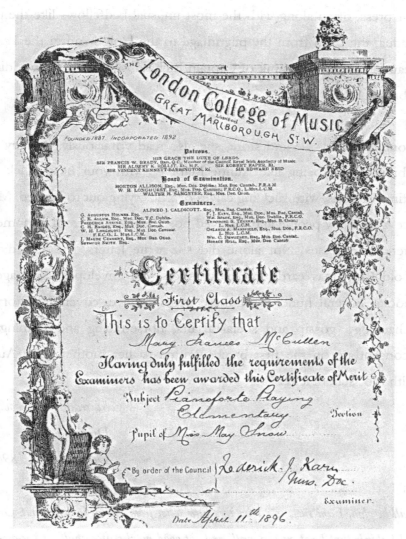

This certificate may explain why Mary was not corresponding regularly with her Aunt!

Chapter Eight
Letters from the Custodian

It would be true to say that none of this book could be written if it were not for the unusual respect given to the written word by Annie's daughter, Mary Frances. The vast bulk of the letters were sewn together in packs, according to author, and carefully stored in some desk, drawer or press, often along with the most unusual bedfellows like the plait of Sister Anthony of Padua, the palm from the pilgrimage to the Holy Land in the 1920s, the coral pieces which came home in the trunk of Captain Richard Moore, or the wedding shoes and bouquet of February 1881.

Not alone did Mary file and store, she also read voraciously, and my father would sometimes upbraid us for being like Auntie Mary – "with your head stuck in a book" , especially at a time of crisis, with suckling calves or kale crying out to be wed. Mary kept up a correspondence with many people and received postal deliveries, from at home and abroad, at several different addresses. Not alone did she write letters, she also did sections of genealogy on old Christmas cards, paper wrappers, old envelopes and pages torn from school copy-books. Several hundred of these items survive, covering history, geography, genealogy, archaeology, gossip and social affairs, horse-racing and farming, but at this juncture, we concentrate on the first batch, written to her mother. Like Aunt Sissy, she commences with the "school letter".

Sacred Heart School,
Drogheda.
December 20th, 1894

My dear Mother,

You shall be glad, I am sure, to receive this little letter from me, as it is my first. Our examinations are now over and I think that I got on very well, and got good marks. We shall get vacation tomorrow and hope the weather will be fine for us to enjoy ourselves. Today the Xmas hamper with some nice prizes will be raffled, in aid of the Holy Childhood. I hope I shall be lucky and win something. As this is my first, you cannot expect a long letter. I will now conclude, wishing you all a very happy Xmas.

I remain, your fond child,

Mary.

December 12ᵗʰ, 1895

I am delighted the time for writing our letters has arrived as it gives me an opportunity of letting you know how I am getting on at my studies…successful…raffle in aid of the Holy Childhood…twopenny lottery…I hope I may get something nice…

While Sister Anthony of Padua was agitating for Mary to be sent to schools as far as Hertfordshire and Galway, to get used to the colour of the Benedictine habit, and perhaps create a tourist trail to Bartestree, Mary was eventually sent to the Loreto Convent School in Navan, which at the time had a direct rail link to Drogheda, passing through McCullen's farm.

Most of Mary's letters to Mother are undated by year, an omission she could not be accused of in later life. It seems likely that she went to Navan in 1897 and graduated to home in June of 1901.

September 25ᵗʰ

The great news is that I was put into Second Year junior grade class by Mother Rosalie and I commenced German also…we were all presented to the Bishop on Monday…a long walk on Wednesday, James' special hatred, I thought very nice…commenced music with a Miss Bennett…very nice…Christina Morrin, stayed with Mrs. Monks, her aunt in Lusk…commenced a tea cloth in Mountmellick work.

Please send me a half-crown P.O. before Tuesday and flannel bodices with 63 and my name on them. You had better come down to see me, or I might get too fond of this school, and might not come back at all…

October 13ᵗʰ

Enclose my monthly marks…the Bishop is now much better, and the Nuns are coming back today…

October 24ᵗʰ

...*Mr. &Mrs. Corry were here on Friday...Cattie Dodd will be coming here in a short time...Is it true that Aunt Cissie only writes to Nuns, now?...I hope the Drogheda Musical Society is a success. Did Father get the English Grammar for me yet?...Sister Ignatius told me to tell you to come before Advent, as you cannot see any of the Nuns otherwise. Do any of the Beabegs ever come down on Sundays? How is Uncle Harry?*

October 2ⁿᵈ, 1897

As James came in this week, you need not expect a very long letter from me. I received the music, shoes and marking ink all right, the ink was a very good kind and just what I wanted, but the shoes are not the right sort, if you could get a pair of black canvas, I would be obliged, if not, you need not send any...Fr. Crean was to call the next day to see me, but he did not...

I was very glad you all remembered my Birthday, John was very good to send me such a pretty picture, and as for Paddie!

November 21ˢᵗ

...*very much disappointed that Father did not come...send me four yards of pink ribbon about an inch and a half wide, a pair of white silk gloves and a pair of <u>nice</u> dancing shoes...Do you hear how Mrs. Reilly or Ida Symington are now?...I am taking a bath every morning now, so you may expect to find me very strong when I go home...*

Undated

...*Last Sunday we celebrated Mother Rosalie's feast day and got out to Delanys. The Bishop brought us over to Athlumney Castle and into the Mercy Orphanage...the Nuns looked very odd, without cuffs...*

November 28ᵗʰ, 1898

...*Please send me the "White Heather Waltzes" by J. Westwood Oliver. I think they are 1/6 in Kearneys...I am glad that the Corporation have a more docile Town Clerk as it would have been inconvenient for them if they could not bring all their grandeur to Fr. Curry's ceremony...Is Anthony talking yet? I am sure he can walk this long time. How is Margaret getting on? Is she in the hospital at present? Please remember me to Catherine...*

P.S. Please send me some chilblain ointment.

November 6th, 1898

Many thanks for the parcel and letters…Father was telling me about all the trouble you went to get one of the books…I saw Ricardo on Tuesday…the operetta is "Red Riding Hood", which they had some time ago in the Sacred Heart School…

December 12th

Many thanks for Postal Order…all about the concert in Drogheda papers…please keep me one of them…did the pictures you sent me last week come from Hereford or Mayo? Tell Joe that I am preparing a good number of new stories for him…

March 5th

…The boots were too large, so I sent them over to Richard with a pattern of the right size to send home in his bags…My chilblains are not as bad as before vacation, although the weather is very cold, we have snow every second day. Which of the helps were invalided? I hope Dominic was not. Is the Cemetery to be on the site Father proposed?

May 1st

…The music examinations are on Wednesday next – say a good prayer for me at 12 o'clock. If Father is not going to Diamor next week, please send me an order for 2/6.

Did you notice any improvement in my writing yet? I suppose you saw in the papers that one of the girls here, M. Ryan, won a Christening cake at the St. Vincent de Paul Bazaar in Dublin…

May 23rd

Please send me 6/ - I want 2/6 for Rev. Mother's Feast day and a small silver locket for a child's birthday – when sending it, do not say what I want it for, or that it is a new one…

Did Aunt Cissie condescend to attend St. Mary's during the Mission? Hoping <u>somebody</u> will keep their promise to come and see me…

November 4th, 1900

I got the portmanteau on Thursday evening when Dick was over – he was in great form and expected to be able to see me next Sunday again…everything here is just the same as usual…no news…unless I take to penning descriptions of the girls, which you would not find very interesting…

November 19th

...I suppose you heard that the Bishop is coming to, or has arrived in, Mullingar...I am very glad to hear that Hal is improving. I suppose the other youth is as extraordinary as ever in the eyes of his Aunt...I would be very glad to get letters from any of the scholars, though I won't promise to answer them...

February 24th

I suppose you consider that Father's visit last week will free you from the obligation of writing to me for the next month but I do not have the same opinion...

If Paddie is not too much taken up with his classical studies, I would be glad to get a letter from him. Are the ladies of the Bazaar Committee having any more entertainments?

I remain,

Your fond child,

Mary.

To arrive home in Summer of 1901, from the ordered academic life of the Loreto Convent in Navan, to the hectic life of a farm with a family of ten and ten workmen, plus a "help" in the house, must have been a dramatic change for Mary. The care of Hal, now aged seven, and Anthony, aged three, would have challenged an eighteen year old girl with hobbies of reading, music and conversation.

As I can testify from personal experience, cooking food for humans was not her favourite occupation, but it seems that her mother had a great way of managing people into their strengths. Almost immediately, Mary took over the bookkeeping and wage-book, and gradually also picked up the job of family scribe to the "scholars" away at Colleges. Richard had announced his intention to his father in 1897 to be a priest, and pursued that aim from the age of twelve years through the Seminary in Navan, to Maynooth, and ordination in 1909.

While he laboured in the Colleges the letters from his sister give a clear insight into the daily debates, farm work, gossip and local news in Beamore, and also show the rapid maturing of Mary under Annie's tutelage. There are six of these which survive, covering the period 1903-1910.

St. Finian's College, Mullingar. Gymnasium.

"We have loved her in life let us not forget her in death."—*St Ambrose.*

✝

In Loving Memory
OF
Dorothea M. Reilly,
MILLEXTOWN, ARDEE.

Who died on Tuesday the 26th June, 1900.
AGED 19 YEARS.
R. I. P.

✝

A light is from our household gone
A voice we loved is stilled,
A place is vacant in our home
Which never can be filled.

GENTLEST Heart of Jesus, ever present in the Blessed Sacrament, ever consumed with burning love for the poor captive souls in Purgatory, have mercy on the soul of Thy servant, DOROTHEA; bring her from the shadows of exile to the bright home of Heaven, where we trust Thou and Thy Blessed Mother have woven for her a crown of unfading bliss. Amen.

Sweet Heart of Jesus be Thou my love.—300 days each time.

Sweet Heart of Mary be my salvation. 300 days each time.

Jesus meek and humble of Heart make my heart like unto Thine —300 days once a day.

My Jesus, mercy.—100 days each time.

The voice is now silent, the heart is now cold,
The smile and the welcome that met us of old;
We miss her and mourn her, in sorrow unseen,
And dwell on the memory of days that have been.

If love and care could death prevent,
Thy days would not so soon be spent,
Life was desired, but God did see,
Eternal life was best for Thee.

O Lord, Thou gavest her to us to be our joy, and Thou hast taken her back from us, we give her to Thee without a murmur, though our hearts are wrung with sorrow.

LALOR   EARL-ST   DUBLIN

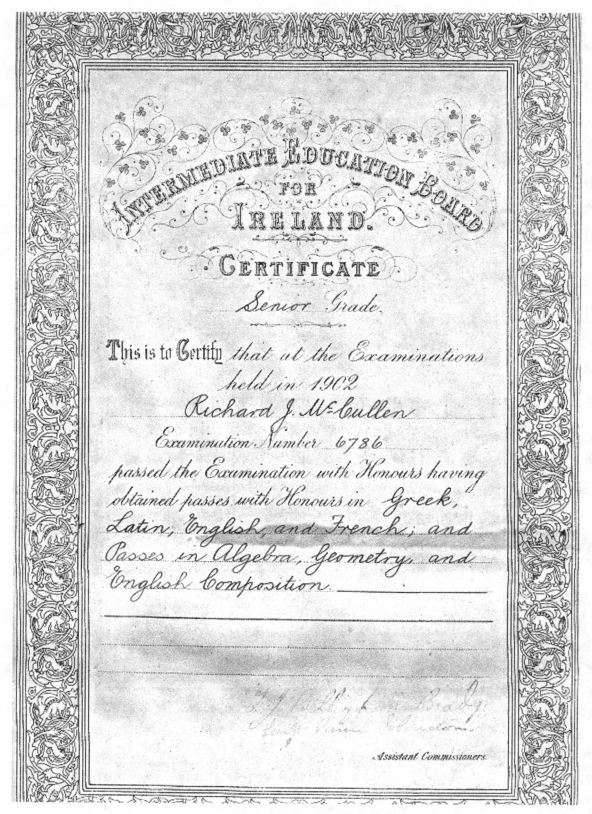

Senior Grade Certificate of Fr. Richard, 1902

Beamore,

January 27th

Dear Dick

    I have looked everywhere for the quotation you mention, but I cannot find who on earth wrote it…Paddy wants to know if you have a Bury's History of Rome…Long got it for South Dublin by 1500 votes. "Boss" Croker late of Tammany who is at present living in Stillorgan lent five motor cars to Hazelton to bring up voters…the gentleman who declared he was not a relieving officer was "thrun" out by his high-souled constituents…"The Freeman" has been making very merry over the failure of the "thirty bobbers" to impress their views on the British workmen…

    It was a pity the donors of the stained glass windows did not encourage Irish manufacture. "The Tower of Glass" in Pembroke road turns out beautiful work, some destined for Loughrea Cathedral, was exhibited at Ballsbridge Horse Show, was really splendid…

    John wants his tea now, so I must stop. He has had toothache on and off for the last week, so Pa thinks it is a case for intervention of "Web-foot", alias Connelly.

    Mary.

March 4th, 1903

My dear Dick,

    …Hal took the measles last week from Anthony and is still in bed with them. All the children of St. Mary's and adjoining parishes seem to have resolved to settle the attendance problem by going on the sick list, some favour measles but the majority favour whooping cough.

    "St. Stephen's" is unusually good this month. Cruise O'Brien is the president editor. He is also Secretary of the Young Ireland Branch of U.I.L. – the time he can spare to his studies can't be much.

    A Dublin barrister named Byrne took the prize at the Theatre Royal Pantomime for a lyric –

        "If I were Mr. Balfour

        I would, I would

        When sick of Parliamentary life,

        I'd stick to golf, and seek a wife

        I would, I would."

and so on.

The Protestants are putting up a little wooden hut for S. Cooper. We had a visit from Mr. Parr, Sen., who is superintending the job and Peter Farrell who is attending the putter up, of said edifice.

The Saw Mills is about to be closed up…it is said that F. Smith is going out to his brother in law in America. I was in Navan, and saw a youth giving the gates of the Seminary a kick, clearing the chasm on his way to McGillicks…

May 8ᵗʰ, 1904

My dear Dick,

…Poor Jas. Reilly died at Stillorgan and was buried in Athlone. Thos. McCourt was buried the same day in the new Cemetery St. Mary's…died of congestion of the lungs. You have doubtless heard of Mr. & Mrs. Macken's marriage. They are at present stopping at Laytown, and intend residing at Bryanstown when that dwelling is done up…Father and James were in Mullingar Fair last week but did not go to the dedication ceremony…then the Pater patronized the M.G.W.R. for Ballinasloe…

Last week, I read J. Eliot's "Mill on the Floss" – it's a wonderfully able book. Almost all the minor characters belong to the one class of people, rather stupid, very honest, and intensely middle class and narrow-minded, in their ideas, but still each one has an individuality of its' own. The King and Queen did not call on you this time, as far as I can see, their visit has been something of a fizzle. E. Delany's mare, St. Corrine won some great race at Punchestown. The King was greatly struck with her and offered Edward £2500 but the latter, wanted £3000. Of course, all this must be taken "cum grano salis".

We are all very busy boiling all kinds of things for a calf afflicted with an interesting disease known as "Timber Tongue"…nothing further to relate.

Your affectionate sister,

Mary.

Junior House – Maynooth, photographed 1902-'03

(Meath Rhetoric, Logic and 4th Theology and Monitor)

L. to R. front row – J. Tallon, J. Kelly, C. Murtagh, T. Keappock.

L. to R. back row – W. Swan, P. Giles, M. Downes, D. Smyth, R. MacCullen, M. Hughes, P. Connell, P.Lennon.

December 5th, 1904

My dear Dick

...Beginning at the wedding – I did not see it, as I was in bed with a bad cold...the attendance rivaled that of a last night of a mission..."Boiler" had a tall silk hat and was best man...Lizzie and Katie went with Mattie and Mrs. (McC.) to Miss Carroll's marriage with Davy Sheridan...it was a very swell turn-out, one of the clergy present was from Castleknock!

I was at a performance of Hamlet in Theatre Royal – house packed. Hamlet & Polonius and gravediggers were very good, the Queen only middling and Ophelia good only when she went "dotty", as P. Guilfoyle put it. James was in Ayr & Glasgow last week...the only topic of conversation in railway carriages was the "free kirk" and the "wee kirk" questions...

I read Johnson's Life of Grey...his criticisms of G.'s poetry are too ridiculous for anything and he seems as cocksure as Macaulay about everything. John wishes me to tell you he hasn't time to write to you anymore…Mr. McDonnell of Kilsharvan died a fortnight ago, and the attendance at the funeral was very large, including Fr. Curry and Fr. Clavin…Paddie is imploring me to remove the <u>*two obstacles*</u> *to his peace, to bed, so I conclude, Mary.*

P.S. P. says there is a son of the "Leader of the Irish Race at home and abroad" in his class at Univ. College.

THE UNDYING OATH.

In June, 1795, Wolfe Tone, Samuel Neilson, Thomas Russell, Henry Joy M'Cracken, and other patriots, assembled on MacArt's Fort, Cavehill, Belfast, and there took a solemn oath never to desist in their efforts until their country should be free.

Dungannon Club Series.   *Printed in Ireland.*

Surviving example of Dungannon Club cards

December 8ᵗʰ, 1906

My dear Dick,

Will you please send me a complete set of the Dungannon Club Postcards (not written of course). Emily O'Reilly is going to Irish classes in Rathgar – she says Dr. O'Daly is an ideal teacher…Now that the purchase of Reays has left us municipal rate payers, I'm thinking of joining the free Library…The Cardinal revoked his panegyric of last Easter, and now seems to regard the Libraries as "a compound of the seven deadly sins with a dash of bubonic plague thrown in".

Mr. Egan, Miss Durnin's husband, seems to be determined to make things hum in Beamore. He intends to stall feed and is building a shed for the purpose. As we are at present using the cultivator in the Road field, you may guess that every brick that goes on is carefully watched. The Irish Unionist alliance had a meeting in the Rotunda…the "Great Irish" poet Edward Dowder presided. Balfour had intended to come but then he funked.

Mother says you may expect a letter and remittance in a few days, so that you won't have to work your passage home. At present, there is a strenuous campaign being opened on Reays – fencing, gates hung, posts sunk, etc.

James and my Father are going to a fair in Limerick on Monday.

Yours,

Mary.

February 18th, 1908

My dear Dick,

The only books I have had out of the Library are Scott's Peveril of the Peak, and Old Mortality and two books on St. Patrick. Old Mortality is really a good book…

When driving up to Salmon recently, Father, J.A. and J.K. stopped to inspect the ploughing match at Gormanstown. Everyone expected that Tommy, alias Mouse, Markey would take first prize, but he only got second, a ploughman of McKeevers of Elm Grove taking first. Mother and Anthony were in Dublin last week and visited the new Art Gallery…

Harry Mallon and Kirwan intended leaving this year but have since reconsidered. T. McCann, J. Moore's boy, has had a very bad attack of pneumonia and is in the Cottage Hospital…the lambs are only making their appearance just now, Turlough was tied up early in the week…Mother and Father saw Paddie last week…Mr. Ginnell is still in jail…the despot of Prince's Street will retire from chairmanship of the Freeman as soon as he can. As you may guess, Father's feelings on the subject are simply indescribable, I think he'd like to choke the three head participators, Redmond, Healy and O'Brien…

Has your book appeared on the world yet? Joe is warning me, so I must desist –

Yours, as ever, Mary.

"The Spirit of the Lord is upon me; wherefore He hath anointed me to preach the Gospel to the poor. He hath sent me to heal the contrite of heart."

—*(Isaias LXI., 1.)*

A. M. ✠ D. G.

A SOUVENIR

OF MY

ORDINATION TO PRIESTHOOD

AT

MAYNOOTH COLLEGE,

ON

JUNE 20th, 1909

(Feast of the Purity of B.V.M.)

AND OF

MY FIRST MASS,

CELEBRATED ON

JUNE 21st, 1909

(Feast of St. Aloysius Gonzaga.)

RICHARD J. MacCULLEN.

"Do this in commemoration of Me."

Ordination Card of Fr. Richard, 1909

March 10th, 1910

My dear Fr. Richard,

Teresa's business will be up again on Friday week...James was down to Nenagh Fair with Mr.

Grey, a Protestant farmer from Ardee. According to him, North Louth has not settled down since the

Election, and both parties are canvassing like mad for the next one, Healy did not get a vote South of Dundalk, while Cooley and Ravensdale went solid for him...

Jack McAuley has got himself into a pretty tangle over some grass he took lately at Monasterboice. Immediately adjoining it live a number of very small farmers who raise cabbage, job in cattle and do a variety of other things. They had expected to get this piece of land cut up between them. McAuley took the hay of it last year, and could not get it made up. It is lying there still, rotten. Lately he put in cattle which were promptly "driv". Fr. Carolan, the P.P., thinks this was not done by any of his lambs, but according to James, this colony of Balgathern jobbers are capable of anything, "from murder to missing mass".

Father had a coat built for himself in Crotty's, something on the style of yours. Anthony has been left at home by a severe attack of complicated chilblains. Paddie prescribed some solution for them and the bandaging and dressing is quite an operation...John is still camping in Salmon. Since Xmas, some carpentry, but no plastering has been done yet...

Col. Brodigan died quite suddenly yesterday in Piltown. One of the Staffords is in command there at present, as none of the Brodigans are home — Mrs. is in the Isle of Wight, the son in India, and the daughter in London!

As ever,

Mary.

As you may have noticed, "Dick" had become Father Richard, after his ordination in 1909, and Paddie had become a Doctor in 1910, so he was able to prescribe for all the family ailments. Both of these achievements were a source of great satisfaction to Annie.

Years later, when in his nineties, Father Richard asked me were the furze bushes still growing in the Long Leg field near the pond.

"Oh, yes," I answered.

"That is where we hung Mary's clothes to dry, after she fell into the pond!"

"Who pushed her?"

"That is classified information, young man."

Peace had broken out between the top three of the family, so we now examine the writings of Paddie, John and Joe...all with a mind and spirit of their own.

Fr. Richard and Mary F. McCullen,
pictured on May 15th, 1961 at Crofton's Hotel in Dublin

10—176.

𝕿𝕳𝖊 𝕹𝖆𝖙𝖎𝖔𝖓𝖆𝖑 𝖀𝖓𝖎𝖛𝖊𝖗𝖘𝖎𝖙𝖞 𝖔𝖋 𝕴𝖗𝖊𝖑𝖆𝖓𝖉

MEETING

FOR THE

CONFERRING OF DEGREES,

SATURDAY, OCTOBER 29th, 1910, *at 3 p.m.*,

IN THE UNIVERSITY, EARLSFORT TERRACE,

ADMIT BEARER.

Entrance by Door A   (11.) 2,000. 10. 1910.

Chapter Nine
The Three in the Middle

John Alphonsus McCullen,
pictured on the day of his First Holy Communion, aged 10 years

My father used to tell us a true story about his two adjacent brothers and himself, which is so typical of three boys with only two years between the middle and the other two. A group of calves were kept in Clinton's field which was one field away from the yard and also required a crossing over the stream known as "The Bog". Paddy was a very clever student and highly motivated, and at the stage of this saga, was travelling by train to Dublin on a daily basis. In those days, crossing the fields for a short cut to the Station was commonplace. At the lower end of the yard was a deep ditch, which took water from a spring in the Well field, and also any run off which came from the grain pits, sheep dipper and various heaps of farmyard manure. A heavy plank about nine inches wide spanned the ditch and was part of the short cut.

One evening on his return from the train, Paddy was crossing the Bog and noticed that the stream was milky-white in colour. He was afterwards a very astute diagnostician and was in the process of developing powers of observation to a high degree. His deduction was that some persons had been sent with buckets of skim-milk to feed the calves in Clintons, and tiring of such menial tasks, they had opted instead to spill the stuff into the stream and let it flow towards the sea at Mornington. Being a highly principled young man, and perhaps even realizing the polluting value of milk, he reported the matter to the Authorities in Beamore. Thereupon an official inquiry was held and the two culprits, John and Joe, were identified, and in John's own words, "We got socks!"

This "socks" was painful, so the two lads met afterwards to devise a scheme of retribution on their big brother who would be running for the 6a.m. train on the following morning. They got a saw, and cut through the middle of the plank crossing the mucky ditch, until only a small piece remained uncut. The devious scheme worked to perfection and Paddy ended up in the smelly effluent and muck, with his good clothes and, worse still, his bag of books. In the Household scale of values, books ranked very near to the top, so there can only have been more "socks", but we never discovered the exact nature of the punishment. I can imagine that Annie probably said that the plank needed replacement anyway.

Paddy's ease with learning and science did not absolve him from farming and one undated reference in a letter of Annie's states – "Paddy was sent to stay in Diamore till the hay is in there." In the surviving bundles of letters, it is clear that Paddy was very focused on his studies and school activities and was not noted for writing long epistles. A letter from Annie to Richard, in December 1903, clarifies this matter rather succinctly.

My dear Richard,

…Paddy surpassed himself in writing last week as we received about <u>five lines</u>, and to make it more provoking, there is a long description in this week's Leader of a hurling match between Newbridge and St. Colman's, Fermoy, and then he says he has no news!

With best love, as ever,

Mother.

There seems to have been a strong connection between the Moores and the Dominican Order, and Henry McCullen the Carpenter had been asked to provide help in making an artistic wooden frame for the Rose window of the Dominican Church in 1870. Aunt Teresa also had a loyalty to the Order for some reason – you may recall Mary F.'s query in her letter of 1899 about whether her Aunt had graced the Mission in St. Mary's with her presence. Paddy had been christened Patrick Dominic and Teresa was his Godmother, so he was sent to Newbridge College with a character reference from the Prior, after a spell with the Christian Brothers in Drogheda. One letter survives.

Coláiste Droichead Nua,

Saturday 10th.

Dear Mother,

I received your welcome letter this morning. Richard looks very well, and does not seem to be overburdened with hard work. The College is magnificent, especially the Senior Chapel. As the matriculation course is very easy, I am doing the honours course in Latin, French and English and Mathematics, with the first Arts lads.

The teachers (for University only) are

Eurelle (or something like that), M.A., English, Latin & French

Connolly, B.A., and medallist through all the Intermediate Grades at Arithmetic and Algebra

McGhan, at Natural Philosophy and Euclid.

As Sunday was Rosary Sunday, we got a walk to the Curragh (we only get walks on State Occasions) and went through the whole Camp there.

I got the bike on hire in the town, paying 6d for the half day — something like 20 lads went. Four fellows came here during the week, one from England (Whitehaven) and three from Kerry.

Hoping you will write soon,

I remain your loving son,

Paddy.

Reports on P.D.'s progress occur regularly in letters from Annie to Richard, who seems to have been a particular confidant of his mother's. Of course, Mother Anthony of Padua also had her eye on him and remarks in a letter of November 7th, 1907, "I am very pleased with Paddy, he is so good and so unassuming, I hope he will succeed."

October 1903

…I was in Dublin, and slipped down to Newbridge to see Paddie. I was startled to find him only after getting up. He fainted on Saturday night and felt a pain in his side after. He remained in bed and fainted again on Sunday night. He was visited by two doctors, and both said it was the effect of a chill. He said he was all right and left me to the train (only he felt weak after being in bed) and expected to go to class next day. I am very anxious till I hear again from him.

May 1904

…Paddie was on the team of hurlers who went to Fermoy (to be beaten by four points). They left Newbridge at 8, changed once at Mallow (where a man pursued Paddy when crossing to the other platform, told him he knew his Father and Mother well and that his name was McDonagh or McDonnell). Were in Fermoy at two. Left at nine, reached Newbridge at four. Went to bed, slept till tea, and went into class!…

February 1907

…James spent a night in Paddie's hospitable quarters last week…Paddy protesting that he'd have to pull up by hard work and study, for the time he was devoting to him…

April 1907

…James inveigled Paddie to cycle yesterday to Salmon thence to Fairyhouse, and home. The latter pronounced the excursion to be a "blooming fraud". He means to return to Dublin on Monday, proceed to Maynooth on Tuesday and you are to be prepared to receive him at about 12.30.

October 12ᵗʰ, 1907

...*Mrs. John Moore, Duleek St., presented a daughter to Mr., so Mary and Paddie were called on to act as sponsors on Thursday last (the first time they so acted) and the Rev. T. Keappock performed the ceremony (for the first time, he confided to Paddie) but Fr. O'Farrell was also present. The young lady was called Dorothy Frances* (afterwards Duffner).

November 27ᵗʰ, 1911

...*The Doctor looks thin, but is well. He attends in Dublin so frequently now that we don't see him often, besides he is getting more to do since the cold weather set in. We have his pony here for a rest, and the Grey is again on duty.*

Paddy became Doctor Patrick McCullen, finally, in September 1910 and went off with his references to seek a position.

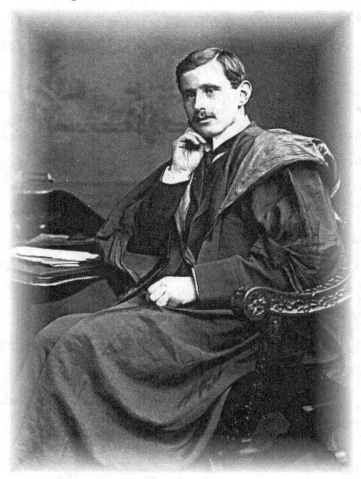

Dr. P.D. McCullen

(COPY.)

35 *MERRION SQUARE,*
DUBLIN,

October 4th, 1910.

I have known Dr. Patrick McCullen for some years, and it gives me great pleasure to bear testimony to his merits, both personal and professional.

Dr. McCullen has had a most distinguished course in the Royal University and Catholic University School of Medicine, gaining many important distinctions in each. From my personal knowledge of Dr. McCullen in the Mater Misericordiæ Hospital I can certify that he possesses a sound practical knowledge of medicine and surgery, and that he is thoroughly competent from every point of view to discharge in a satisfactory manner the duties of any medical post.

MARTIN DEMPSEY, M.D., F.R.C.P.,

Physician, Mater Misericordiæ Hospital; Lecturer and Examiner, N.U.I.

42, Merrion Square,

Dublin.

October 15th 1910.

I have known Dr. P.D. McCullen for some years past during
his career as a student of medicine in Dublin and I feel great
pleasure in stating that I have formed a high opinion of his
professional attainments. Dr. McCullen was a most attentive
student in the wards of the Mater Misericordiae Hospital where
he enjoyed exceptional facilities for acquiring a thorough
knowledge of his profession. He was selected to fill the post
of Resident Pupil and he discharged the duties of this office
for a period of six months in a most satisfactory manner. He
is now fully qualified to practise his profession and I can
strongly recommend him as a well trained practitioner of
medicine and surgery.

JOHN LENTAIGNE

Surgeon, Mater Misericordiae Hospital, Dublin.
Consulting Surgeon Royal Hospital for Incurables.
Surgeon to the Household of His Excellency the
          Lord Lieutenant of Ireland.
Ex-President of the Royal College of Surgeons
          in Ireland, etc.

Star Footballer:

At the age of thirteen, John was sent to the Seminary in Navan, following James and Richard. Like James, his interests were agricultural, but he became another letter-writer. Nineteen of these letters cover 1903 to 1905, mostly sent to his Mother. In the first few days he wrote three letters.

October 3rd, 1903

…I received "La Tulipe Noir" in the bag this morning. A new pupil came, his name is Sheridan, being a brother of Dick Sheridan from Oldcastle. It is a wonder my Father would not call in when he is going to Diamore, as I am lonesome and it might rouse my spirits.

I remain as ever,

John.

P.S. As all my money is nearly run out, please send 2/6.

October 6th, 1903

…Send a looking-glass and a clothes brush and some blotting paper…and some nibs and the rubber. Please excuse me for asking for so many things…I am sending home a boot to be mended, which will want to be done soon. Make a pair of garters for me – you make them to fit Joe. You will find the key of the bag in a stocking near the mouth of the bag…

October 10th, 1903

…I suppose James is busy at the hay in Diamore yet. There are about 79 or 80 students here now. We had the usual walk on Thursday. Ask Joe how are all my companions getting on in the Christians…

I hope Anthony is well these times, did he get his curls sheared yet?

Tell Joe to write soon.

Your loving son,

John.

P.S. I forgot to tell you to stiffen the collars well when sending them. I do not feel the days flying by, and it will not be long until I am home.

The reasons for the boot repair urgency become more clear from a letter written by Annie to Richard.

October 29th, 1903

...*Mary and Joe paid a visit to John in Navan last Saturday...he appears to be becoming more reconciled to his fate, as he says he does not feel the days flying by, and he is the best football player in the "Guff's Team", everyone being afraid of his boots.*

Meanwhile, John continues his on the spot reports from "the prison", as he used to describe it, in later years.

November 28th, 1903

...*I got the parcel from Nicholas Connor on Wednesday...Did anyone go to visit the new place at Balbriggan? A letter from Paddy says a teacher, named Connolly was knocked down by a tram-car in Dublin. I am sure they are very busy with the stall-feds now...Does Joe rather have the Christian's than Scott's? I am sure Mary takes great value from the range...*

Is there any big "gents" about, dying? I suppose you have all the turnips drew in. Did you get the mill yet?

December 19th, 1903

...*You can expect me home on the 4.40 train...Did you get the place white-washed yet? I suppose Joe has great times of it, at home, now.*

One letter, to his brother Joe, is written on a torn piece of copybook, in the same, neat, small handwriting that he was still writing to his own sons in the 1960s.

(Undated)

Dear Joe,

I received your two letters which were very pleasing to me. I suppose you get a great many trips to Balrath, and Balestrand and Bodingstown, now, which save going to school. Have any of the Christian Brothers changed yet? Do you have to go with the milk now? Please tell me if you went to the Show last week. Ask my Mother did she send the Rosary beads, as I did not open the bag yet...

Please buy an India-rubber, and send it in the next letter.

Jack.

In April of 1904, Annie confides to Richard –

We received a card of invitation to "The Pirates" to come off on Thursday night, by the students in the C.Y.M.S. Hall, Navan. John looks very well, but did not grow an inch. Joe is looking down on him now.

And in May –

John said the fire was next his dormitory, that he heard the priests taking out basins of water, but was too sleepy to rouse himself.

Joe McCullen in 1902

In the Autumn of 1904, Joe was sent off to join John at the Seminary and Annie describes the scene –

John and Joe were driven off to the 3.45, in the midst of Monday's storm, by James. John (with a touch of your proclivities having sent his overcoat, in his trunk, by the ten) was drenched before he reached the Seminary, as I learned from Joe's letter received this morning. He also told me the Revd. D. Flynn fell from his horse during vac., was brought home in a coach, that he was kicked badly, and is not able to stir...

Letters from John are almost always dated precisely, unlike his older siblings', and contain snapshots of history as well as his personal requests and remarks.

January 30th, 1904

...The Bishop left Navan on Thursday...send down a bottle of ink and tell Ang to put a cork in it...Do you ever go over to Mount Grandville now? You might send down some cash.

February 20th, 1904

Dear Father,

I thought it time to write a letter to you...I suppose Joe is taken up with nothing only the war, and Antony very busy with the lambs...Tell my Mother to send the envelopes and the unfortunate stamps...Did you go to Mr. James McCann's funeral?...Had Antony to fast on Wednesday, if he had, I suppose he thought it a great honour...

March 5th, 1904

My dear Mother,

Thanks for all my wants and the boxes of ointment...I can imagine Antony herding the sheep and lambs...I suppose the people of Drogheda are all going to observe St. Patrick's Day a National Holiday...

March 28th, 1904

...I was sorry to disappoint Mary and Joe, but was on retreat – I hope they enjoyed their ride. Tell my Father to write to Fr. Flynn, nobody will get home unless he has a letter...my chilblains are nearly all gone...Thank Mary for the cakes sent down to me...

May 4th, 1904

...I suppose my Father is very busy at Salmon, and at home sowing turnips. Does James ever visit Ayr now?...Will I be home for the Regatta?...The weather is intensely warm – you might send a pair of black canvas shoes...

April 9th, 1904

...I may tell you that the play was splendidly acted and I was disappointed at not seeing Mary or my Father down...send some soap in the bag and the Roman History...

April 21st, 1904

...I send a pair of trousers and want you to mend them, and also a pair of boots for mending...The cricket commenced on Sunday...I was surprised James was not down at Navan Races this day week...

May 21st, 1904

I hope Mary and Joe got home all right on Saturday after their fine day's outing...I suppose the people from Drogheda are beginning to stop at the sea...did Joe go for any bicycle rides since?

At present there is nothing very strange about Navan, only that the weather is fine...

November 26th, 1904

I was surprised that you did not answer Joe's postcard during the week...I can't think of any news at all but we can talk a good deal this day four weeks...

P.s. Send Joe's overcoat as soon as you can.

December 3rd, 1904

We had a free day on Tuesday last...The Bishop was in Navan during the week, but as usual he did not come near us...Tell Dick I have not time to write, and not to be disappointed...Tell anyone going to Diamore, to break the journey and call to the Seminary...

January 31st, 1905

...I have a boil on my neck so if you could send a muffler or something of that kind, I would be obliged...a rule was made that everybody would have to sleep in the same place as before Christmas, so Joe got back to Paul, and was surprised not to see the polishing brushes in the bag...No news about here now as it is the same dirty town...

April 1st, 1905

...We had the retreat, it was a Vincentian (I do not know if that is the correct spelling but you know what I mean). You may tell my Father or James that they might not have been so stingy with their *visits, and if they be going the way of Oldcastle, they might break the journey at Navan…Fr. Curry was here on Thursday, and Joe and Paul Kelly were speaking to him – I did not see him…do not forget to send the customary letter to Fr. Flynn to get myself and Joe home for Easter…*

April 12ᵗʰ, 1905

…Send the bag as soon as possible, as I am in very great need of it…send 5/- as Entrance fees for Joe & myself for the Sports…we had a science examination – it was not very hard…It is not worth writing long letters now as I expect to get home on Saturday week. Joe is all right. Hoping all are well,

> *I remain,*
>
> *John.*

By Spring of 1907, John had been moved to live in Salmon, along with James, and Joe was still suffering in the Seminary. Annie records in April of 1907 –

Joseph looks well, but departed yesterday morning in a gloomy mood. He had a very gloomy tale of a pupil who went home the week before last, and died after a couple of days.

The close connection between John and Joe is well illustrated by a visit in 1907. The former, now a fulltime farmer, was on his way home from Oldcastle Fair, with a flock of sheep, assisted by Harry Mallon, and decided to call to see Joe, so they drove the sheep into the gates of the Seminary for Harry to hold up while John visited his younger brother and also caused some excitement in the world of Fr. Flynn and the eighty boarders.

Perhaps this unsettled Joe, or he may have felt sufficiently educated for life, because Sister Anthony writes from Bartestree on November 7ᵗʰ, 1907 –"

I made enquiries about each of you, they say Joe is remaining at home – I am rather disappointed, as from his photo, I expected great things from him, of course he may do well, but then I thought he should exert himself with something else…

Regardless of the Convent view of things, Annie was very successful at guiding her family into roles that suited them. Salmon farmhouse was being mooted for construction, and Joe fitted well into the continuing operation at home. How was Mother Anthony to know that within twenty years, Joe would have more land than any of the others and a wife and five children?

Annie managed to keep herself in touch with the artistic and musical world, as well as political developments and farming affairs and was involved in the Golden Jubilee celebrations of the Convent of Mercy in Drogheda on November 8th, 1904. The programme of events is as follows —

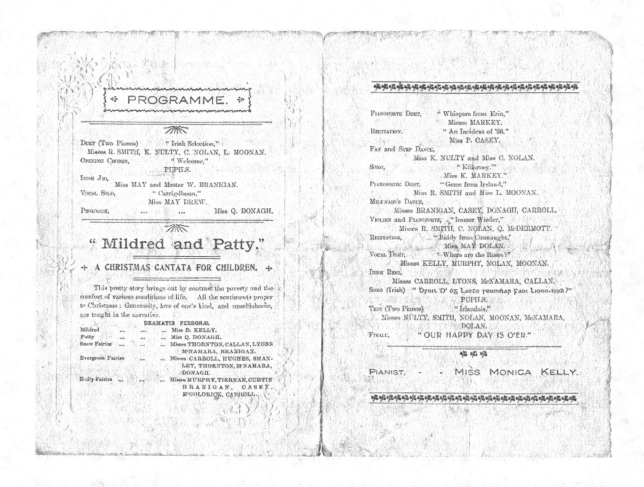

She writes to Richard —

February 2ⁿᵈ, 1907

…The rioting over the play in the Abbey Theatre seems to be dividing public attention with the new Education Project…

April 6ᵗʰ, 1904

I saw a plan of the O'Growney Monument for Maynooth in the "Evening Telegraph" by Mr. Scott Junior, late of Drogheda. (To an untutored mind like mine it savoured of a dog kennel or chicken coop.) Only they are so hackneyed, the Round Tower or Celtic cross seems more imposing…

A MEETING

WILL BE HELD AT

THE MAYORALTY ROOMS,

DROGHEDA.

[By Kind Permission of the Mayor],

On Friday, 20th Nov., 1914,

AT 4 O'CLOCK.

To Organise the Relief for the Belgian Refugees in the Laytown and Drogheda Districts. :: ::

His Worship the Mayor will preside.

The Meeting will addressed by

REV. G. O'NEILL, S.J.,

:: AND ::

REV. FR. MONSAERT.

[Belgian Refugee].

and others.

EILEEN GORMANSTON.
R. E. JAMESON. *Hon Sec.*
pro tem.

Chapter Ten
The Little Ones

Henry Vincent McCullen, Hal

There are certain jobs on a farm which require extra help, such as branding with a hot iron on the horns of the animal and castration of stirks, or six month old bulls. When these situations arose, and my father, John, was past retiring age, he would summon help from Kilnew. This was the farm where his youngest brother eventually was settled and in the fifties and early sixties this brother had a fine, strong son to accompany him. My father would say, "Here comes poor little Anthony and young Paddy!" The same poor little Anthony was six feet tall and built in proportion, and I often wondered why he was described as "poor" and "little". The adjectives can be explained by his position in the family. He was Annie's youngest child, born in January of 1898, four years after the birth of Henry Vincent, known as Hal. Hal was mentally handicapped and must have absorbed all the care and attention that his mother bestowed on him, while Anthony was very precious because he came later, was healthy and was the baby of the family.

Richard decided to become a priest, walking on the Beabeg road, and announced his decision to his father outside Mrs. Connor's house (now Larkin's). This was in 1897, and Annie supported him in every possible way, as well as confiding in him, through her letters, about her anxieties, and the progress of "the younger fry" as Mary Frances used to describe them.

It is very possible that Father Curry of St. Mary's was very interested in the "boyos" at the Seminary in order to secure vocations to the priesthood, or indeed because of shared political views with "the Boss", or perhaps just as part of his role as Parish Priest. There is an interesting letter from him to Pat.

> *St. Mary's,*
> *Sunnyside,*
> *Drogheda.*
> *February 7ʰ, 1902*

Dear Mr. McCullen,
    The Bishop of Meath will address the Congregation in St. Mary's on Sunday next at 11.30 on the subject of the new Cathedral. He has intimated to me his desire to have the names of parishioners who are

likely to give him respectable subscriptions, before Sunday, and I write to you to express the hope that you will do so, and to let me know the amount you propose giving before Saturday evening.

I don't expect ever to officiate in the contemplated building, but I suspect some of my parishioners, including a number of your family, will. When that day comes, you will rejoice that you have done a man's part in erecting that great temple for the service of the living God in your native diocese.

With kind regards to Mrs. McCullen and wishing you and her, and all the family every blessing.

I am,

Dear Mr. McCullen,

Sincerely yours,

John Curry.

The Bishop in question was Most Rev. Matthew Gaffney who actually resigned in 1906, due to ill health, and died in 1909. The collection of funds to build the Cathedral continued until the dedication of a new building in September 1936. Father Curry was long dead, but Father Richard MacCullen did officiate there.

The great expansion in building of churches, convents and schools in the last thirty years of the nineteenth century was followed by their decoration and embellishment in the first two decades of the twentieth century. A letter came on February 14th, 1911, from the Augustinian Priory in Drogheda.

Dear Mr. McCullen,

For the sake of old times and your connection with this Church in the past, I feel you will send me a small donation towards the payment of our debt. There are so many collections in Drogheda of late, that I am compelled to appeal to the charity of outsiders.

I am sending you a paper that will explain why this debt was contracted.

Yours faithfully,

E.J. St. George.

A year later in February 1912, Fr. Curry was working energetically on the interior of St. Mary's Church and his list of contributions received to date, for 1911-1912, was printed and circulated, in the hope of eliciting further contributions from other parishioners. The monies received are listed, in descending order, from Mrs. Mathews from Mount Hanover with £25, to four names with 2/6 each. Pat McCullen fits into the £5 category and Desmond Drew told me that his father Johnny was "held back" at an enthusiastic meeting by Pat, who counseled him to wait until the money promised reached "our level".

Some interesting subscriptions are –

Servants, Kilsharvan	5 shillings
The Military, Millmount	£3-11 shillings

Father Curry kept working on Pat and Annie, and the Mosaics, as a reredos for the High Altar, were a separate collection. The third picture "Behold the Lamb of god" was erected in memory of their parents at a cost of £43. The inscription reads, "In memory of James and Anne McCullen and Richard and Mary Moore, R.I.P.".

Henry Vincent

He was called after his granduncle Henry who lived in Beabeg and had a large family, dying in 1903. The handicap meant that he required a lot of minding, and also was prone to pick up infections, particularly respiratory ones. Annie brought him to Dublin for extra treatment on a regular basis, as soon as he was able to travel.

Hal seems to have been very attached to Richard, and in a letter of January 1st, 1905, Annie writes to Richard –

...I enclose the catgut as directed, the Bishop's letter is very strong, and arrived very speedily. Well, Hal did not finally give you up till after John and Joe's departure.

Now and then, his condition is referred to, in the letters of both Mary and Annie; Mary, writing to Richard on November 22nd, 1907, says –

...John, Mother, Anthony and Hal have been suffering from a sort of intermittent influenza for the last fortnight. John was in bed for a few days last week, Anthony and Mother ditto this week, while Hal passed the entire fortnight lying before kitchen and parlour fires alternately. We are all very dull without Paddie...

In the same letter, she turns to matters agricultural and observes –

For the last few days, we have been anxiously expecting the mill to return, but the bad weather has hampered the mill owners everywhere, and it is very difficult to get even a promise from them.

Osborne has three mills working up the Co. Dublin since the season commenced, while all his neighbours had to call in Co. Louth mills. Coming down from Balbriggan lately, he told James he did not want to be bothered with the Shallon farmers as they never paid, either in cash or kind...

By 1910, Annie and Patrick had decided that Hal, who was now sixteen years old, required some further education and engaged in a correspondence with the Brothers of Charity in Belmont in Waterford. Simultaneously, Teresa Moore seems to have been in some trouble in the Public House in Duleek Street. The troubles were financial, and one of the causes may have been her own consumption of alcohol, and a refusal to "take her share" of the business and move out of the Pub. This latter choice was the one suggested by Sister Anthony of Padua, and by Annie and Pat some years earlier, and not acceded to. The two issues, of the Pub and Hal's further education, are covered in a letter to Richard.

Beamore,

March 11th, 1910

My dear Richard,

Yesterday a letter arrived from Mattie (McCullen – cousin) *saying O'Brien wanted to see one of Miss Moore's sureties this morning. Mattie couldn't, Father wouldn't, so James went, and we received enclosed telegram. Bennett's valuation of premises was £650. She has a fortnight now to procure sureties who mean to dictate stringent terms and accept no risks. I hope she'll submit quietly now.*

We had a long letter from the Superior in Belmont this morning saying he had received a reply from Ghent where there is a house of the Order. They have a young man in Belmont who spent four years there. The pension is £24 per year. If we incurred the expense a brother would come to Waterford for him.

In haste, Mother.

Teresa's case came to a head in the following year when Tom Callan was installed as a manager of the public house, and he eventually purchased the premises at public auction in 1920. One of the conditions of sale was that Teresa Moore be paid ten shillings per week for her life, which he continued to dispense until she died in 1946, at the age of 84 years.

Hal left home to become a residential pupil with the Brothers of Charity in 1911. Once again, Annie writes to Richard –

November 27ᵗʰ, 1911

…I felt much disappointed at hearing from the Pater that Antony is not applying himself to his work as closely as he should. Mrs. Lynch tells me they sent their boy to Clondalkin. Only I have so much occupation, I would feel very lonely as Mary has been in Salmon <u>since the treasure left.</u>

James and John come down occasionally but Joe is the only fixed resident here now.

As ever,

Your loving Mother.

After some time in Belmont, Hal moved to the Strop, a residential home in Ghent, Belgium, and the publicity brochure still survives. When war broke out, Father Richard and James went to Ghent, with much diplomatic preparation because he was moving into the area of battle, and succeeded in extricating Hal from the Strop in order to bring him home. This was quite a perilous escapade and, in later years, Father Richard, who had an eventful and long life, often spoke of the trip to rescue Hal, and amongst his documents were the bundle of permits from the War Office in London.

Hal did not survive very long at home and must have been shattered by the loss of his mother. He died in March of 1916, within nine months of Annie.

Anthony Joseph McCullen

Anthony

There are very few surviving letters to or from the curly headed youngest of the family but every now and then, his mother passes on the latest interjection or appearance by him in the kitchen. These most often occur in her letters to Richard.

.

November 29th 1903

...I enclose a letter from Ang (the pet name) which I was told not to read, I do not believe you can, either!

(Undated)

...Poor Ang set off yesterday morning all impatience to go to school, but last night confided to me that he would not go anymore, that it was all a "cod", tiring yourself going there and making an elaborate toilette, and much better to learn your lessons at home. So he went off reluctantly today.

November 5th 1904

...Aug came in to tell me that "if Paddie and Dick want to see the machine shearing, they had better come home, quick." Shearing, turnip sowing and going to fairs are the order of the day at present.

October 2nd 1907

...James, Mary, Joe and Anthony were at the Drogheda Show on the second day. V. Hoey and Rooney, Beamore were amongst the successful owners of jumping horses...I was in the Convent re knitting on Saturday and was getting bagged making all kinds of lame and impossible excuses and explanations for your remissness in not visiting during vacation...

When Richard was ordained, he spent a short while as a "supply priest" in the parishes of Dunboyne and Mountnugent, during the summer of 1909, and was then appointed on September 13th, to succeed Fr. Lynam, as Professor of Greek, at St. Finians Seminary, now based in Mullingar. Anthony was a student in the Seminary at this time, so Annie had a view from both sides of the fence in the College. Clerical appointments became a more interesting topic of correspondence.

October 15th 1912

My dear Richard

I send the jersey and hope that the sight of it may impel you to take a trip...Please give enclosed note to Anthony. There is a rumour afloat that Fr. Dunne is leaving here for Trim...

The Bazaar Ladies are surpassing themselves moving about in all directions on bicycles. If it is kept up at the same rate for the year, we must expect gigantic results. "Festina Lente" seems still the motto of the Curate's Stall as I did not receive any tickets till this morning. Preparation for a Dance before Advent being set on foot in connection with it…Is it your Fr. J. Kelly who might be coming to us?

Best love, as ever,
Mother

In spite of the "Festina Lente" policy the "Dance" turned into a Masked Ball which was held in the Mayoralty Rooms, Drogheda in 1912, in aid of the Church Fund Stall presided over by Mrs. McCullen and Mrs. J.A. Clarke. The decoration was carried out by Messrs. Davis and Co., and music supplied, in first class style, by Dermody String Band, Dublin. A report of the time states - "There were memorable scenes in the Ballroom after the unmasking, when the countenances of the ladies were revealed in all the glow of animation and beauty."

Despite Anthony's lack of application in November 1911, he was still in the Seminary twelve months later, and one letter to him from Annie, survives -

Beamore
December 8ᵗʰ 1913

My dear Anthony,

I suppose you are all getting ready for St. Finian's this week. Joe has been in Salmon last two weeks, since the cattle went in. Christy hurt his foot and is supposed to have gone for a rest. Mary and John enjoyed the lecture on Lourdes, given by Father Norris very much. Mrs. McCullen (Beabeg) is going on well - of course Paddie sees her every day. I think Father R. would not make a wrong shot if he thanked Mrs. Clarke, Bryanstown and Miss Green, North Strand, for the cushions, as they were the only two who were most anxious about him in the Bazaar. The mantle drape won at our stall by Fr. Clarke has been got from him and is to shine again at the Dominican…The bees are well, and devouring the bee food. The Pater is in Granard today.

Best love, as ever, Mother.

It seems most likely that Anthony returned to Beamore in 1914, at the age of sixteen to add to the farming brothers, now numbering four and with lands to be farmed at Beamore, Bryanstown, Clonlusk, Salmon and Diamor. A substantial farm at Bodington, Clonalvey and a farm of 50 acres at Ballestran, Stamullen which had been rented for some years were let go in January 1907 in order to concentrate on Salmon and Bryanstown (Reays). For whatever reason, the farm at Diamor, Crossakill, of 217 statute acres, was transferred to Joe in 1912, who was then aged twenty. Plenty of responsibility at an early age seems to have been the policy of Pat and Annie, in dealing with their family. Some of the Bryanstown lands were transferred to Anthony, but he was in no great hurry to establish a permanent base, and when he did marry Johanna Sheridan from Giltown, in June of 1931, he had already purchased in 1930 a fee simple farm at Kilnew, Clonalvey, from Joe Dwyer of the Bull Ring in Drogheda, and eventually settled there.

Bearing in mind that Annie had lost the favourite brother, Richard Moore to the "angry sea" at the age of twenty-nine, in 1885, it must have been a great occasion to her when Richard was ordained on June 20th 1909. In much later life, he was noted for the brevity of his communications, and when I requested that he officiate at the wedding of Ann and myself in 1966, he replied saying "Too far, too old, much too much to eat, leave it to Dick" RMcC. At that time he was 81 but still functioning fully as Parish Priest of Kells and Vicar - General of the Diocese of Meath. In 1909, he writes –

> *Maynooth,*
> *The Morrow of the Ordination*

My dear Mother

Business first, Dawson says he sent on the bicycle on the 15th June; queer: let him see to it. Today, I said my first Mass here, all right for all in Beamore. I am not rightly recovered from the drunkenness of yesterday's joy; all I realize is that there are others in the same position as me. I am told that it is the joy of a lifetime, so let me enjoy it while it lasts.

They are having the D.D. Concursus today in the Aula. The younger members of the family will be pleased to know that the objectors (8 of them) representative of religious orders and theological faculties are xxxx & Revd. "Dinny Flynn".

The results of the B.D. are out. I have held my place pretty consistently. Out of 16 candidates, 11 are through, 5 stuck.

Walsh (Meath) leads

Keogh (Kildare) No.2   } *both these headed me in dogma since we entered Theology*

Connell (Meath) No.3   }

McCullen (do.) No.4

So you see, that the only effect of not killing myself was that I got 4ᵗʰ instead of my usual 3ʳᵈ place. Some two mistakes, one rather unfair, brought me down a bit in the important subjects, but the secondary ones stood to me, like Church History and Scripture.

R. MacC.

P.S. I'm sure the Bishop is delighted with 3 places out of the top 4.

It is interesting that Richard uses the classical phrase " the drunkenness of yesterday's joy", because one of the items discovered tucked away in a book after his death in 1977, was a certificate of membership of the Pioneer Total Abstinence League, dated 3ʳᵈ November 1905, and signed at Maynooth by. P. Coffey, Promoter. He had been a Pioneer for 72 years, but often dispensed a drop of whiskey to his guests.

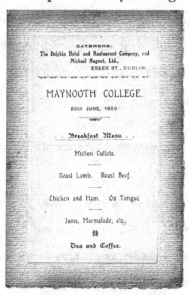

CATERERS:
The Delphin Hotel and Restaurant Company, and
Michael Nugent, Ltd.,
ESSEX ST., DUBLIN.

MAYNOOTH COLLEGE.
20th JUNE, 1909.

. . Breakfast Menu . .

Mutton Cutlets.

Roast Lamb.   Roast Beef.

Chicken and Ham.   Ox Tongue

Jams, Marmalade, etc.

Tea and Coffee.

Chapter Eleven
A Time of Change

Annie Moore McCullen

You may recall that after the loss of her "treasure", Annie expressed the opinion that she would be very lonely, but for all the occupation that kept her mind off it. Apart from the domestic scene, the never-ending bazaar for Saint Mary's, the several correspondences and the caring from a distance for her absent sons, she had a keen political sense. Writing to Richard on May 20th, 1907, she sums up the Irish Question –

…Your Father had a copy of the Bill from the House of Commons immediately after being issued. Mr. Moore and Mr. Ward (Duleek st.) and Mr. McKitterick, Solicitor, are the Drogheda delegates. I am afraid if the arguments become physical, one muscular patriot from the Western World will overcome our representatives. Like everything British, it is a huge fraud, but many people think it wise to accept it, as it may be getting in the thin end of the wedge. Bill Murray will represent the Foresters, another case of good goods in small parcels.

Father Doran was here yesterday and, for a man of peace, talks in a very belligerent way of the Bill. Of course, it all proves the infallibility of Mr. O'Brien and Tim Healy. He hopes it will be fully discussed, while Fr. Curry has declared confidence in John Redmond and John Dillon and Co. Peace and <u>unity</u> at any price.

Well, another piece of news – the Editor of the Argus asked your Father to write another letter, which he declined doing, with a superior air, remarking he was not paid to educate the Drogheda Corporation…

Ever yours,
Mother.

In a similar fashion, Annie kept herself up to date with the artistic world. Reporting on local drama to Richard in March 1908, she writes –

…Mary and Joe were at the "White Horse of the Peppers" on Patrick's Night, performed in the Town Hall by the National Theatrical People. They enjoyed it very much, of course. The Company could not get a theatre or an audience in Dublin while Burns and Roche were performing…

We are to have a Station on Saturday next. The latest report is that the Old Chapel bell was stolen from Sunnyside last week…

Best love, as ever, Mother.

Annie was in her late fifties and still keeping up the busy, active life, but her health was not as good as it should have been, and Sister Anthony writes, in 1913, that with the Bazaar now finished, her "fatigue" should be lifting. This fatigue must have got worse, and complete rest away from home becomes the cure. The place chosen to provide the recovery is Kilkee, in County Clare, a seaside town, and eight letters and a postcard remain, which she sent to Beamore while on an extended holiday. Replies are also extant, from Mary and John. This particular correspondence begins in July of 1914.

> *Rock Lodge,*
> *East End,*
> *Kilkee,*
> *Co. Clare.*
> *Thursday evening.*

My dear P.

I reached here about 6.15 and Paddie was waiting on the platform and conducted me here. A road and low wall only separates the house from the Atlantic (as if the River at Laytown opposite Kennedys was the water of the ocean). As he says the post leaves here at five, you will scarcely receive this till Saturday. He then went to dinner at seven but will return in an hour. He met Mr. Doyle, the Christian Brother who is in Ennis teaching, but here for vacation. My tin of Brands bread and butter and a few chocolates made a splendid dinner before we reached Limerick. Then I got a tea basket of nice tea etc., and amused myself with it, from Ennis to Kilkee, so that I feel quite independent. It was well I brought them from home, as I could not get anything till the tea basket.

I hope everyone is well — tell Mary that I had not any very interesting fellow travelers, but escaped some puffed up things in the next compartment.

With best love to self,

And each, as ever,

Annie.

Kilkee Co. Clare.

This postcard was sent to John on July 12th, 1914 and her message reads –

Pin hole through window of present apartment. Excursions from Limerick for football match, in field to right of this house. Good breezes today. Got "Independent" of yesterday but no communication from home yet. Remembrance to all. Quite well.

There are three remaining letters from Rock View Lodge, two to Mary and one to Pat, and they are quite comprehensive.

July 11th, 1914.

My dear Mary,

 I presume Paddie left by seven o'clock train this morning, as he intended last night. Of course, he will give full particulars of the locality when he reaches home. There is a bay, formed by "the Ocean" as the youngsters say (they never call it "the Sea") with a little semi-circle of sandy strand between two rocky promontories. The houses are around in a semi-circle.

 Then you have the primeval and extra modern extremes, with everything jumbled between. Tell Anthony there is no cinema, but we have swinging boats and a Theatre with the Queen's Co. performing nightly. Daily Mass at eight but there are two others as well. Tell John the bread is delicious in bread carts, exactly like Drogheda carts, about the size of a Bacon box drawn by donkeys. The water is brought in barrels on Donkey carts and delivered by the bucket. There was a fair here today and I went through the cattle twice when going to Mass. They were much more respectable animals of all ages than the Balbriggan exhibits. I suggested to Paddie to invest in some, as there appeared to be no buyers and that we might have a profit, but he was afraid they might be like Dr. Burke – Savages investment. I saw a man at the hotel door, looking at them, and thought it was James at first. Well, it turned out there were no buyers only Conner from Cork and they would not suit him.

Turning to the residents of the house, it belongs to a shopkeeper in the town. The housekeeper appears to be of the B. Mitchell type, the servant is from Dublin, but graduated in Blackpool, London and, of all places, Ballybeg with Lady Trimleston. She thinks she would like France next, but dislikes Frenchmen. There is a lady from Limerick, with nurse and three small children, two of whom are really interesting. The Mamma might be a sister of Mrs. J. Moore, she is so like her.

Now, I hope you are all very well. I am getting on nicely but was disappointed in "the Ocean" which is now just as calm as the Sea at Bettystown. The wind also has been from the east since I came, and is a mild soft bog wind. Father Rooney of Longwood is expected here on Monday to the Hotel. Dr. O'Dwyer was down from Limerick in the train I travelled by; he is very cross looking!

Give my love to each. I hope the Pater got home safe on Thursday. I need not tell you how I am watching to hear from home, I suppose tomorrow.

As ever, dear Mary,

Mother.

Rockview Lodge,
July 14th, 1914.

My dear Pat,

I received your, Mary's, and Fr. R's letters and "Independent" this morning together. I need not tell you they acted as the best tonic yet, as I was somewhat dismal on Sunday and Monday. I felt like a little four year old girl staying here, who asked the postman if he had any postcards for her? "Cross old thing would not answer me, I'll write to the Postmaster General." So you do not have a patent!

Of course Paddie gave all particulars of the locality, manners, habits and customs. I think the dining facilities here will tempt his Rev. from Lisdoonvarna, when he arrives in Clare. Diving and bathing seems to be the occupation of one half of the population and watching them at it, the job of the remainder. The East Enders don't approve of Golf; the Links are situate in the back of the West End.

When coming down the street with a paper yesterday, I saw a crowd of children congregated, and walked on through them till I saw a swarm of bees, on a low wall beside the footpath, someone had partly covered them with a costume box, but I did not delay to take a second look. The people staying in this house are booksellers in Limerick (tell Mary the Mrs. is evidently taking a holiday from books and papers. Mr. Hannon drove down in a motor car for the week, and accompanied by a Fr. Moylan of the African Missions in Cork. On Sunday evening, they had to take Mrs. for a drive. They very kindly invited me to accompany them and we went to Doonbeg, which is a curiosity here as the coast is like Mornington, with sand hills. We saw the Volunteers at drill in the village, with a priest in their midst. They all had wooden guns. I have discovered a Provincial Bank, a United Irishwomen's depot (very shabby looking), a Presbyterian church, a photographic studio, an "Ocean View", which looks into the windows on the opposite side of the street. The people here say I look improved already, but I think it is only sunburn. It is too soon to give an opinion yet, myself. Tell Mary I enjoyed her long letter, and will write soon. Best love to all,

Annie.

July 23rd, 1914.

My dear Mary,

I received the letter of yesterday from Father and will not decide on any change till I hope I will see him, on Saturday. Fr. R. will I hope remain until the 6th of August. The Limerick people left on Monday and I enclose sticky back of the Nurse and children. There were new people expected yesterday and when we came in at two o'clock we met a bag of golf-sticks in the hall, next we saw the Irish Times, and then we heard the name was Carter of Ennis, so we deduced "sour face". This morning he told his Rev. the Golf Course was rotten, lost three 2/6 balls there yesterday evening, played a season in Limerick, and lost only one; there is a lady and two children attached.

You would want two complete outfits here, a tropical one for the eastern and an artic one for the western winds. I had to put one skirt over the other today. I send some rock garden specimens rooted up in a square yard of the farthest projecting head here. You might make one or two grow. Anyone who bathes and swims here seems to scare the golfer who of course does nothing but golf.

There are great regrets here at the removal of a curate Father Maloney to Kilrush as he had established a band which performs frequently, and is very good, he also formed the Volunteers. There is a Nun airing herself about, dressed like a Mercy, only the black veil is lined with pale blue and she wears a thick purple girdle; she seems to be with the same lady and gentleman frequently.

How are you getting on? I hope all are well. I suppose pressure of business prevents John or Anthony from writing a line. One of my chief occupations is watching the postman on his two rounds.

Mrs. Harman's husband used to have to write to her <u>twice</u> daily or she would nearly get hysterical, then she'd have telegrams as well.

I have been repairing the overalls this morning where they were splitting here and there. I hope Jane and Jack are assisting you effectively. I will make you laugh when I go home, about the helps here. The Cook sent in a message, with the dinner, yesterday to me —

"to ring like the dickens, when we had the soup finished."

Best love,

As ever,

Mother.

One of Mary's replies is still available and she has written on the top beside the date "War was declared that day".

Beamore

August 4th, 1914.

My dear Mother,

You must forgive me for not writing on Sunday, but James came down and I did not like to start writing as John and Anthony went off to the football.

Martin Knight came over on Wed. last and took out three sections of honey. He says the bees are doing well in the new hive, that they have a queen but that he will leave them the rest of the honey for the winter. Miss Jameson of Delvin was married last week to Capt. McDonnell of Kilsharvan, while Miss Jameson of Platten is getting married today, to Farrell. I am told the date of this marriage was anticipated owing to the mobilization of the forces. All the Navy Reserve men left Drogheda on Monday morning. A good many went from Paddy's district (about Francis st.) and a great number from Clogherhead.

John is very anxious to know if his Rev. went to Tralee on Sunday for the football. Smith of Colpe did not go.

Please tell us if you are going to remain in Kilkee for the entire month. Candidly, I'd advise you to, because nothing round this side will do you as much good, and we are getting on very nicely as it is.

The post is going now so I'll have to wind up.

Love as ever,

From Mary.

Annie returned to Beamore at the end of August 1914, but her condition did not improve and so she set forth to Kilkee once more at Easter 1915, in order to find a cure in the Atlantic breezes and a place of rest. This time she resided at Pink Lodge, from where she writes to Pat.

My dearest Pat,

I got down all right yesterday and Miss Keane sent a man to meet the train last night, who took the bags here. There were two ladies in the carriage with me, leaving Dublin, one disappeared at Nenagh, the other came as far as Sixmilebridge. I took possession of a compartment; on moving into West Clare, at Milltown-Malbay, they slipped off three carriages again, I had a compartment to myself, then on changing at Moyarta myself and belongings were put into an empty compartment (I think they thought I had one engaged). I saw your old reprobate of a ship beached up there, but...dotted with a couple of islands and a craft the size of one of the old Drogheda Colliers, with rowboat attached, proudly floating there; this lake continues to Black Weir. I went for a walk Golf Ground way after 11 o'clock Mass. The Church was filled and the place does not look as deserted as you'd expect. I even saw one khaki-clad individual on the promenade today, the first after leaving Ennis. From Limerick to here, all along the line, everyone has plants down. Everything here is very comfortable, except the front door has to be barricaded against the ocean breeze which causes delay in coming in or out. In spite of the long journey, I am better now than when I was leaving home or leaving Dublin. I hope you and all the flock are quite well. I'll be looking for news from home now.

    With best love to each, yourself included as ever,

    Annie.

The weather was poor and several letters were sent in the following few weeks, to John who replied in some detail and to Doctor Paddie, who was now medical adviser to his Mother.

                                                 Pink Lodge,

                                               Kilkee.

                                     April 7th, 1915.

My dear John,

    This day has been stormy and showery but not so constantly wet as yesterday. The natives are very busy coming with crib-carts to each tide gathering the big leathery seaweed, to clap on their potatoes, no use if they let it dry! When I looked out on Easter Sunday morning, the first thing caught my eye was three gents, towels and all correct, going for a swim. I saw one in the water, but his stay was a short one. Mutton appears to be very scarce here. You have to go from shop to shop looking for a chop. Beef is plentiful enough. All yellow fat, I suppose with Indian meal, as I saw them giving something in buckets in the fields coming along. I have not seen a paper since Monday. When I went this evening, I was told they will not come until the 9.30 p.m. I could get nothing later than a Cork Examiner of Monday, which I declined.

    If you or Anthony would have time to post the "Freeman" at night when everyone is finished with it, I would have it time enough, as they will probably be all sold, when I go in the mornings, but it doesn't matter if inconvenient.

    I hope Mary and Father got my letters. Best love to all,

    As ever,

    Mother.

The reply from John is a masterpiece of his style, and is dated April 9th, 1915.

My dear Mother,

    I received your letter this morning. You would make a great mark as a war correspondent, you can write off so many letters from such an out of the way place as Kilkee. The weather here is very showery and *cold – the well field is beginning to have its usual April look on it, since the beginning of thus week. About news since you went away – Anthony and I went to the Passion Sermon this night week. It was preached in a very modern way by Fr. Coughlin from College Hill, who was in Navan with me. Went to Drogheda in the usual way on Saturday to sell oats and buy seed potatoes, sold no oats and bought <u>two</u> <u>barrels</u> potatoes. Meanwhile, met Joe who came from Oldcastle that morning, coming from Edgeworthstown where he bought 11 cattle.*

My Father and myself went to 11 o'clock Mass on Sunday, saw scaffolding removed and heard it announced that we are to have a three-week mission. On Monday, found that our employee, Mr. McCann, did not turn up to his work, sent Anthony over to his house to enquire for him, to be told he hadn't been seen since the previous day at 11 o'clock. Went over myself to look for him on Thursday, and was told he was working for Mr. McCullen, Mile House.

Proceeded to Drogheda on Easter Monday to enquire the price of Nitrate of Soda from the Chemical Manure Co., and to get foundations for the Bee Hive. That evening Mr. Knight came over, and we arranged the skep, so that the bees will go into the "body-box". Tuesday, went to Drogheda for lump sugar, to make syrup for the bees, with which I am feeding them every night since.

Met one of the Messrs. Carroll of Mornington, brothers to Mrs. F. Moran, he told me he was working with the L & Y in Liverpool, heard the next time I was in Drogheda that he joined the Irish Guards on Tuesday.

On Tuesday night, Anthony and I went out to the Railway at 10 o'clock for some cattle, which were to come from Diamor; as usual, they did not turn up and the next morning got the usual explanatory note from Melia that the postal arrangements were at fault, and that he would send the cattle the next day. Made a further attack on the Railway the next night and succeeded in capturing 11 cattle, 4 of which were calves, that were fed on cows. One calf was so tired that it took us nearly two and a half hours to come from the Station. The others are getting the usual dose of linseed oil and treacle per the "Boss" who is just now very energetic. Himself and Anthony are preparing a drink of oatmeal water to give to a store bullock who dared to stand in the Well field, and not eat hay.

On Wednesday, started an army of stonepickers, but 5 left at nine o'clock, after dinner, three others turned up and worked very reluctantly the next day, when I sacked them all, except two who finished this evening. Anthony is not sorry that they are finished, as he had to stay with them, part of the time.

Went to Drogheda for a short time on Thursday, when nothing unusual happened. On Friday started 2 chaps to drop potatoes, of which nearly half is down.

Dispatched Anthony to Cumiskeys with sheep and lambs, expected him home on the 3 o'clock train, was disappointed that he did not come until the six when he informed me that, as luck would have it, one of the sheep turned her head around to him, bleated and <u>died</u>. He had to go to Salmon and requisition a cart to bring her there.

Jack informed me that young Mullen (Jane's grand-nephew) who was here pulling turnips and listed in November, has just been wounded. I was talking to Peter Cowley on Saturday — he told me he has great wages in Liverpool. One of the Birdies was home from there and has just returned with another brother on Wednesday.

My Father says he might take a trip to Kilkee the middle of nest week. I have handed the matter of your paper supply to Mary, who will send you a "bundle of Daily News" and daily papers. The ink is getting very low in the bottle so it's nearly time that I wound up this weekly communiqué.

I hope you are not too lonesome, I suppose you can't be otherwise, with so few around. If the wind is any worse in Kilkee, nor what it has been here for the last 3 days, you must be hardly able to be out, but if you are improving, what matters.

I am afraid I have been studying Mr. Pepys rather much of late, as this is more in the nature of a diary than a letter. I'll finish up in Hilaire Belloc's style.

John McCullen.

On the same day as John wrote his longest epistle, Annie wrote to her other son, the Doctor.

Pink Lodge,
April 9th, 1915.

My dear Paddie,

It is too soon to report progress, but I am told I look much better. The waves were tremendous yesterday, but that hasn't prevented me going out each day since I came here. It is well I have a cotton ball and crochet needle to occupy my time during the showers or I might be tempted to carve my initials on the furniture but I am very comfortable and have the undivided attention of the hostess. Have the recruiters and the V.C. left town yet? There were two German young men staying in the house last July. On their departure, the hostess asked if they'd return next year. Their reply was, "You'll never see us again Ma'am." So I suppose they don't mean to invade <u>this</u> coast.

There were two porters, with brass labels on their caps to meet the train at Lahinch but I saw only four probable trippers alighting and none carried golf sticks. The porter who met me and carried down my luggage was anxious to know how long I'd stop; on getting an evasive reply, he remarked that he supposed "as long as the money 'd last". As they speak in a very loud tone, and this was coming along the street, it was decidedly awkward.

> *Goodbye,*
>
> *As ever,*
>
> *Mother.*

Four days later, Annie replied to John -

> *Pink Lodge,*
> *April 13ᵗʰ, 1915.*

My dear John,

I am sure since the Mission began, things are humming at home, to catch up everything. I think it is Anthony I have to thank for the "Drogheda Independent". If it's the least trouble, I don't mind if they are not sent, all the news can keep till I go home. If anyone dies, I suppose you'll let me know. The newspaper shop only has placards of "Irish Times", "Irish Independent", "Daily Sketch", and Southern papers. The poor Freeman is brought straight from this train to each house where it has been ordered.

By the way, the Leader bulged its way, through the Freeman, and had to be roped up in the P.O. There was a fair of little pigs here today, all going home in the donkeys' cribs; prices £1 for 7 week bonhams. They are very smart asses; would make a show of Mick (?). Then Mr. Robinson had the town placarded, that he would be in Kilkee today from 12 to 2, to buy a large number of horses. They have no market day here, but loads of hay and turf come every day, and stand in the square. There are forty pubs, with a population of 1661. I saw two carts out on Sunday evening gathering the seaweed. I hope you will not have got stung, stall-feeding the bees.

If possible, let me know when the Pater will arrive, as I'd like to meet him. I suppose he would be looking for a pink house, while this is <u>cream</u>, with a pink one on each side!

Give my love to Mary as well as everybody else,

> *As ever,*
>
> *Mother.*

After the visit of the "Pater" to Kilkee, Annie moved home to Beamore, where she stayed until May 17th, 1915. Her health did not improve, and it was decided to do further medical treatment in Dublin.

I am coming home by express from MULLINGAR

Postcard from Richard to Paddy on May 15th, 1915

Father Richard came to see her, from Mullingar, on May 16th, and she went to Eccles Street Hospital on the following day. Anxiety over Hal and his future weighed heavily on her, and eventually the medical decision was that a colostomy should be carried out. This procedure precipitated toxaemia, and Annie died, in the company of Pat and the Doctors, at 10.30 p.m. on Sunday, June 20th, 1915. Her sixty years of life had been packed and hectic and the letter of her sister, from the convent in Bartestree, summed up a general consensus.

If I do any good in this life, it is to Annie I owe it; a more devoted daughter, sister, wife and mother could not be.

Pat left the hospital at midnight and, in an effort to come to terms with such a huge loss, walked the city streets of Dublin until dawn on Monday, June 21st.

Chapter Twelve
Pressures of the Time

Looking back a distance of almost a century, there are obvious pressures that must have caused great anxiety to Annie in her final years. The most immediate of these would have been the health and future of her "treasure", Hal. As far as they possibly could, Pat and herself had provided for his economic well-being by setting up a trust fund in 1910, of various investments, to ensure an income for him. His education had been progressing well at the Strop School in Ghent, until the outbreak of War necessitated the rescue mission, by Father Richard and James, into the War Zone in August 1915. It is not clear whether Hal returned to Belmont after being brought home to Beamore, or not, and for whatever reason, he only survived his Mother by nine months, dying in March of 1916, at the age of twenty-two. This may have been a normal life expectancy for a person with his handicap. Having lost so many of her brothers, sisters, cousins and close friends in her own life, it was a blessing that all her eight children survived her. There is an interesting postcard sent by Annie to Doctor McCullen, Stedalt, Stamullen, Balbriggan, Ireland in the 1911-1913 period.

Monday - Bruges.

Met Messrs. White, Connoly (?) O'Brien – had tea on terrace. Father discussed political situation from every point. Crossing to Ostend delightful. Hal, as usual, in Ghent. Fr. R. had left address in Bruges for us. Met him at Benediction in Cathedral. Saw procession, with Benediction in street after. He leaves here for Hereford tomorrow. We are very well, but heat trying.

Mother.

The anxiety over Hal being marooned in Ghent, in her final days, must have been great for Annie. However, the travel permit granted to Revd. Richard Joseph McCullen, Catholic Priest, British Subject, by Sir Edward Grey of the British Foreign Office had come on December 22nd, 1914, and the actual arrangements to travel were not finalized until August of 1915.

Give us Irishmen

At the outbreak of hostilities on August 4th, 1914, Home Rule for Ireland was thought to be imminent by a large section of the population. However, it had been in this "almost there" state for decades, and impatience with the British was growing. You may recall Annie's remark in 1907 – "Everything British is a huge fraud".

As the War progressed, the market for horses and agricultural produce improved, but so also did the "market" for young men capable of bearing arms. Annie had seven sons, two of whom, Richard and Hal, were unlikely to get involved, but the five other young men aged from sixteen to thirty-two, would have been suitable for General Kitchener, and the War Office.

Thus, when Annie asked in her letter of April 1915, "Have the recruiters and the V.C. left town yet?" it was more than just a snippet of news she was seeking. There was always the possibility that one of her sons would, like Jonny Doner of years before, or her own two seafaring brothers, "take a notion" of joining up. In his letters, John mentions local lads who suddenly did so, while Mary reports the rushed marriages of the Miss Jamesons to Officers who were about to be drafted to the Front.

The Campaign

Three documents which were in Mary's cache of letters from the period, give a clear indication of the atmosphere created by the British Administration in the period 1914-1915. Part of the campaign was to create fear amongst a prospering farming class, that the Germans were coming to grab good Irish land.

This is typified by the speech of Mr. T.P. Gill, Secretary of the Department of Agriculture, headed "IRISH FARMERS – every one of your farms is carefully mapped and recorded in Berlin."

THE RECRUITING SERGEANT.

IRISH
Farmers

Every one of your Farms is carefully mapped and recorded in Berlin.

Extracts from a speech by Mr. T. P. Gill, Secretary of the Department of Agriculture.

TO-DAY the farmers are the owners of the soil; they are the rulers of the country. Landlordism is gone; the Grand Juries have given place to the County Councils; bigger legislation has passed. There is nothing like it in history.

Now, all this time, almost coincident with each great Irish measure, there has been a series of legislation in Prussian Poland, the object of which has been, not to root the native occupier in the soil, but to root him out of it, and to plant a Prussian in his stead. The latest of these Acts was passed in 1908, the year preceding Mr. Birrell's big Land Act.

We would have to go back in our history to the Plantations of James and Cromwell for a parallel to what these Prussian-Polish measures signify, and all this is being done in violation of solemn obligations to the Polish people under treaty. For some years past we have had many German gentlemen studying our conditions in Ireland—some of them openly, economists and professors and administrators (I confess I have entertained and piloted some of them myself—returning compliments received when I was at the same business in their country), and some of them secretly, who were installed for long periods in important points of observation here at hotels and elsewhere.

Gentlemen, every one of your farms in the Golden Vein and on the warm Tipperary hillsides is carefully mapped and recorded in the archives in Berlin, and our margin of 40 per cent. and more of insufficiently utilised good arable land—they have no land like it in all Germany—is hungrily estimated in the interests of an overflowing population fighting for places in the sun.

You are happy to-day in your vesting orders under the Ashbourne, the Wyndham, and the Birrell Land Acts ; but let the Germans break the British power and come to Ireland and your vesting orders, like another solemn document and like the Polish guarantees, will be but so many " scraps of paper " in the hands of the Prussian bureaucrat.

Issued by the Department of Recruiting for Ireland, *32 Nassau Street, Dublin.*

(1773.)Wt. — .360,000.12/15.A.T.&Co.,Ltd.

Lord Wimbourne follows this up – The Department of Recruiting for Ireland, November 27th, 1915.

THE DEPARTMENT OF RECRUITING FOR IRELAND.

November 27th, 1915.

Sir,

The year that has passed has seen 100,000 Irishmen forsake civil life to take up arms overseas in defence of the lives, the livelihood and the land of those they have left behind.

Since my first letter to you enough men to form six complete Battalions have rallied to the support of those Irishmen who have already joined.

This is the answer to those who understood Irishmen so little as to think that they could be misled into questioning the high motives and the intelligence of the men who first listened to the call.

It is a splendid response also, to their countrymen in the ranks of your historic Regiments, who have said:—''Give us Irishmen to be beside us, to hold what we have won, and to win on,'' and to their Officers—and not Irish Officers alone—who have said:—''Let us have Irishmen to lead and Irishmen in support.''

The Country's need is still great—more and more men are required—and I come to ask for ''a free gift from a free people.''

Let your free answer be as your conscience dictates. But remember that those who attempt to throw doubt on the peril of the present war to the lives and homes of Irishmen and Irishwomen; that those who spread mean suspicion on men in authority and on the thousands of brave Irish soldiers who are sheltering us; that those who find lame excuses to prevent themselves or to prevent others from fulfilling a hard and noble duty to Ireland—those men censure the dead and insult the living.

I desire to make it clear that my appeal for recruits has been prepared without thought or anticipation of compulsion.

Yours faithfully,

Wimborne

Lord Lieutenant of Ireland and
Director-General of Recruiting.

And then finally, the Prime Minister himself, from January 4ᵗʰ, 1916.

DEPARTMENT OF RECRUITING FOR IRELAND.

The Prime Minister, in his Statement in the House of Commons on the 21st December, 1915, urged upon every eligible man, whether married or single, the necessity for immediately coming forward in the service of his country.

With regard to the single men the Prime Minister said:—

"It is reported to me from many quarters that there are parts of the country where the young unmarried men have not come forward as they should have done in response to the national call. Do not let it be supposed that I— or anybody else—am making any charge against them as a class. Nothing is further from my thoughts. I venture to say this, and I say it with as much earnestness and emphasis as I can command, that those who have been disposed to hang back, whether for good or bad reasons, even now should seize the opportunity of following the example so patriotically set to them by the great mass of the community."

In order that every eligible man may now follow that example, a form of voluntary undertaking to join the colours is being issued throughout Ireland.

A form for your use is enclosed. If you are willing to do your share, whether married or single, fill it in, sign it, and post it. The envelope need not be stamped.

4th January, 1916.

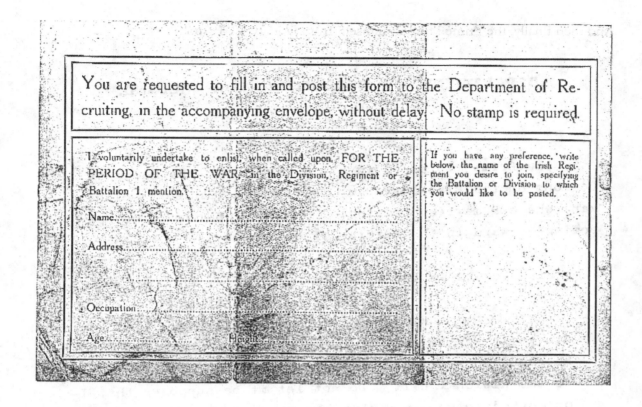

You are requested to fill in and post this form to the Department of Recruiting, in the accompanying envelope, without delay. No stamp is required.

I voluntarily undertake to enlist, when called upon, FOR THE PERIOD OF THE WAR, in the Division, Regiment or Battalion I mention.

Name.......................

Address.......................

Occupation.......................

Age.................. Height...........

If you have any preference, write below, the name of the Irish Regiment you desire to join, specifying the Battalion or Division to which you would like to be posted.

While all this recruiting campaign was going on for a War in Belgium, Ireland itself was also in an uneasy state, with Home Rule at last on the statute book, but not implemented, and the Ulster Volunteers threatening Civil War if it came about. The Southern Volunteers were just as adamant that Home Rule must happen, although their arms were often made of wood, as opposed to the Unionists who had successful and flagrant gunrunning expeditions in 1914.

It is clear from Annie's correspondence that she was very aware of the political situation in Europe, and also in Ireland, and the possible effects on her family and their futures. In addition, travel to see her sister in Hereford had also become more risky. When the split in the Southern Volunteers happened in 1915, a minority became the Irish Volunteers who rejected any form of support, as recruits or anything else, for the British Government, and these were the forerunners of the 1916 Rising. Of the sixteen arrested in Drogheda at Easter 1916, at least twelve would have been very well known to Annie, and based in the Duleek Gate area. She must have been concerned that some of her own lads might be drawn into such a movement.

The V.C. referred to in Annie's letter from Kilkee is Drummer William Kenny, who received the Victoria Cross for his bravery at Ypres on October 23rd, 1914, and was made a Freeman of Drogheda on the following St. Patrick's Day.

Thousands of townspeople were at a reception on the Mall to honour the now Lance Corporal Kenny V.C. and amongst the speakers were Captain Bellingham and the Mayor, Luke Elcock, an old friend of Pat McCullen. A report in the Drogheda Independent of March 27th, 1915, states that "the Captain was accorded a most enthusiastic reception from the immense crowd" and in his speech he said "I am doing my very best all over the county to try to bring home to young men the necessity for their joining the colours…my wife says it is my duty (hear, hear!) and I would ask the women of Drogheda to tell their menfolk that it was their duty to join the colours." (applause)

Postscript on joining up

At this remove, we do not know what Annie might have made of developments in 1914-18, but it is interesting to note that the Anti-Conscription meeting held on the same Mall in 1917, had as one of the principal speakers a young priest named Father Richard McCullen.

The Convent Pressure

An exquisite card with a lace of very fine design on the front cover, is amongst the bundles of correspondence. On the cover is a poem with alternate lines in red and blue ink. It is signed "Pray for Sr. M. Agnes." The first verse conveys its subject matter very clearly.

Come, while the blossoms of thy youth are brightest,
Thou youthful wanderer in a flowery maze
Come, while thy restless heart is bounding lightest

And joy's pure sunbeams dazzle in thy ways,

Come while sweet thoughts, like summer buds unfolding

Waken rich feelings in thy careless breast,

While yet thy hand the fancy wreath is holding,

Come, and secure interminable rest.

Referring back to the Lizzie Donor letters, you may remember the constant querying to Annie, about <u>when</u> she would enter a convent. The pressure on Mary Frances to follow her Aunt May, or her father's two cousins, the Miss Sheridans, into a convent, must have been substantial. Nobody could say that Sr. Anthony of Padua Moore did not try her utmost to have her niece schooled in England, or at convent schools where she would get used to the cream-coloured garb, but hope seems to have faded, eventually. In a letter to Richard while he was in Maynooth, Sr. Anthony says –

November 7ᵗʰ, 1907.

…Mary is not much changed, she is very interesting and I think enjoyed her visit. I do not think she will be a nun. She would feel the pressure of Novitiate very much but if once past that few years, what a splendid subject she would make. She has such a large mind and so discerning, and yet with it all great simplicity. We must however leave these matters in the hands of Him who knows best how to guide us.

*   Sr. St. Anthony of Padua Moore.*

A few years pass by, and Sr. Anthony is still working on Mary, so she writes a long letter of convent news to Mary on January 22ⁿᵈ, 1913.

…It is so difficult to get subjects for the Novitiate, especially in England. Our dear Mother will be regretted…she was kind and considerate to all, and a native of Co. Wicklow…with regard to the Elections, I am anxious to hear the result and we are burning a lamp in the Laundry for the same intention, if successful, you will, I am sure, send on the papers…it is now snowing, we are very fortunate to have the hot pipes.

*   Sr. M. St. Anthony of Padua Moore.*

P.S. Who is the Miss Usher, who has joined the Cross and Passion Nuns?

At the age of 85 years, Sr. Anthony was still observing, and commenting, from behind the grill of the Convent window, and little did I know that I myself was being commented upon, until I discovered a letter of March 1951 to Eva McCullen, wife of Dr. Paddy- in which she remarks- "We saw where John McC and John Drew got distinction at the Fancy Dress Ball for the Sienna Convent - I am glad the sale was a success."

The Miss Sheridans

When Pat McCullen was growing up before he became "The Boss" his home was shared with a maiden Aunt Jane, and a married Aunt, Mary McCullen Sheridan. This latter had married Patrick Sheridan, a widower, who had come from Cavan, and rented land in Beamore from James McCullen, the builder. By repute, Patrick Sheridan was a difficult man, and his wife was wont to fill her mouth with water, so that she resist the temptation to answer him back. They had two daughters who were somewhat younger than Pat McCullen, and their names were Mary Anne (or Belinda Maria) and Bridget. The Sheridans left Beamore sometime before Pat got married to Annie Moore, and took a farm at Donacarney on the road to Bettystown. The mother Mary died in December 1883 aged 50 and is buried at the McCullen plot in Kilsharvan. Mr. Sheridan, as my father used refer to him married a third wife named Catherine, and eventually he died , possibly as a result of a fall from a rick of hay, in September 1919. His daughter by the third marriage was Catherine who herself married John Monahan and the Monahan family continue to farm in the area.

The two older sisters decided to enter the Mercy Order and travelled to a Convent in Ballinrobe, County Mayo. Why they did so is not clear, but a portion of the land at Donacarney was sold to provide their "dowry". Growing up in Beamore in the 1940-1950 period, there were nuns and convents to be visited on both sides of my family, and I was unaware of the Miss Sheridans of the past. In 1984, I published a history of the local St. Mary's Church and parish and include in the appendix, a list of the nuns born in the parish. I also included a chapter on priests born in the parish, and researched a short life of Father James Monahan (1929-1980) from Donacarney, a son of Catherine and John. A month after the book launch, the sacristan, Philip Pentony, stopped me and said that a Mrs. Butterly had left a note for me in the sacristy.

Assuming that this had to do with her query as to the Christian names of the two Miss Sheridans, I phoned Mrs. Butterly and we had a long chat and I made some notes on the piece of paper about where Patrick Sheridan was buried. Almost twenty years later at the commencement of this volume, I suddenly realised that I had omitted the two Mercy Nuns from Ballinrobe, from the list of Nuns born in St. Mary's Parish, and she was trying to let me know about the gap! Even though they were reared in my own home, I had left the two out, so now they deserve a special space. The difficulty was to find information as all I had were sparse notes, and bits of memories from my father's conversations about "Mr. Sheridan". In addition, there were two picture postcards of Ballinrobe, "Wishing dear Pat a very happy New Year", but unstamped. One of these is reproduced here.

Bridge Street, Ballinrobe.   *Co. Mayo.*

As is often the case, Auntie Mary came to the rescue and I found another bundle of letters, including photographs of Mary Anne and Bridget Sheridan before they entered convent life. The one with the dark waistcoat and leg of mutton sleeves is Bridget, the younger of the two.

Bridget Sheridan

Mary Anne Sheridan

There is a long letter which appeared in Chapter Five from Pat McCullen to Annie, referring to Mary Anne's reception in Ballinrobe, on the day before he bought 30 cattle in Balla, but it is undated, presumably in the 1880s, because he requests Annie "to do the best you can" until his return from the West.

There seems to have been a pattern that Pat, or his sons, when visiting the Co. Mayo in search of cattle, sheep or horses, would include the Mercy Convent at Ballinrobe in the itinerary. A letter of sympathy to Pat on the death of Annie is dated June 23rd, 1915.

...on the death of poor gentle Annie, an excellent wife and mother. We were very grieved when we saw her death on Tuesday's paper which our priests send to the Convent, since this fearful War commenced...we have all got to go the same journey...so pray don't lose time fretting, your loss is her gain. Love to you all, your affectionate cousins, in J.C.

Srs. M. Magdalen and Sr. Elizabeth.

Mercy Convent, Ballinrobe

The few letters that remain are all written by Sr. Magdalen (Bridget) and portray a lady who already has one leg in Heaven.

December, 1927

My dear Pat,

How will I even thank my friends in Beamore and Beabeg for all their kindness to me on the death of poor dear Sr. E. a few days ago. Before she died, she expressed her desire to see Fr. Richard and we tried, but in vain, to put her off, so Revd. Mother thought it well to gratify her wish, and let him know, so he came on the Saturday before she died and gave her the last absolution, and she was so happy after she left — may God reward him for his kind act…She wandered a good deal during the end, and all about Beamore and Mile House…poor dear soul, she was a patient sufferer for a year and a half. She got a cold in August 1926 down in Lecanvey and it turned to pneumonia…she was happy to go, and suffered from heart trouble, asthma and a complication of diseases…I got a surprise when Revd. Mother told me Henry and John was come, I could not believe it as the weather was so bad, we were snowed up and we could send no wires, so few priests could come to the Requiem…poor Maryanne, the first of the three of us to go to Heaven, it won't be long till we are all together. Now I feel lonely…am glad you are keeping fairly well, it is as much as we can expect now, as it is growing late.

Now, I wish you all at poor dear old Beamore the blessings of the holy festive season…
Your affect. Cousin in J.C.,
Sr. Magdalen.

Srs. Elizabeth & Magdalen Sheridan

Writing to Mary,

Tuesday, June 14th, 1932

My dear Mary,

You are good to send me that paper and monthly. They are very welcome to an old idler who does very little except read, say my prayers, and walk about the garden on observation duty...I read about poor Mary Woods' death, may she rest in peace...how short is life.

Today is the races day of Ballinrobe, it is very warm, as soon as the staff was taken off, they started sport, you would be surprised where the people got the money.

The Pope seems very anxious about the state of the world...very uneasy about Ireland, holy though we seem to think our people are, none are free from the power of evil, we must pray...I hope to be in Heaven to look down on the tops of the towers in Mullingar. The Bishop of Meath will leave some work for his successor to do...we are mending an old Cathedral in Tuam, as best we can...

Sr. Magdalen.

In February of 1932, Paddy McCullen, a son of Joe, was drowned in a freak accident on an iced-up lake at Hartlands. He was nine years old. The last letter Sr. Magdalen wrote was to express her sympathy to the family.

February 6th, 1933.

Dear Mary,

I was very grieved to read about the death of poor little Paddie – it was the mercy of God they were not both lost, Poor Joe and the Mother, I do feel for them...

Am writing from my bed, where I am for the last fortnight laid up with a bad attack of inflammation of the stomach – I will give my prayers for you all.

Not able to say more,

Sr. Magdalen.

An added line by Mary states – "This letter reached Beamore on Tuesday 7th February. On the next day, Sr. M. died." A telegram to that effect is also appended.

Mary's Vocation

You could say that there was considerable genealogical pressure on Mary to enter the convent life, and when I interviewed Mother Malachy, who was the doyenne of the Mercy Convent in Drogheda, in 1984, she told me that Mary would have joined up, but for the other vocation of looking after her father and brothers. In a letter of June 1915 to Mary, Tilly Collins, living in Bray, but from the Sign of the Knife and Fork, in Shop street, writes –

It is a hard, hard trial to the little girl your Mother loved so well. How proud she was, Poor dear Mrs. McCullen, she always told me, of your brilliant school career, when you passed all Exams.

When you examine the chronology of events after she left the Loreto in Navan, and returned to Beamore and all its frenetic busyness, it is easy to see how Mary's loyalty to her mother, in health and later in illness, and to Hal, and then to her father and brothers, gave her a full occupation. It also left her in a position of Librarian, Archivist, Correspondent, Conservator, Almsgiver and "Aunt" to a large family, who did not always appreciate her talents. In order to catch some part of this complex and influential personality, I include a poem from "Jingles of the Harness", published in 1999.

Travelling Aunt

Now Towell was a soldier from Somerset
"But please, Auntie Mary, could we ever get…"
After the Rosary, child, let us begin,
There's a few trimmin's we have to fit in.

Now a Darcy from Platin came from Dunmoe,
"But please, Auntie Mary, this time can we go…?"
Not without sunhats, down to the field of hay,
You could just catch cold in the sun today.

Now Cromwell brought in a Fellow named Naper,
"But please, Auntie Mary, what was a flapper…?"
Well young idle women with nothing to do…
As I said, he settled down in Loughcrew.

Now the Rath's have a fishcart in Clogherhead,
"But please, Auntie Mary, all fish tastes like lead…"
Never mind child, we'll have some in milk today.
I'll make a nice stew, still fresh from the say.

Now the Boss used to go to Doctor Chance.
"But please, Auntie Mary, did you ever have romance…?"
Tush, child, I looked after the two men,
They needed cooking and minding, now and then.

Now the bowsies haven't sent my dividend,
"But please, Auntie Mary, can we have a lend…?"
You wish to buy comics or books in the shop,
Of course, here is a florin, watch out for Pop.

Now Taafe, evicted from Sillery's places,

"But please, Auntie Mary, can we go to the races…?"

Don't be gambling money, watch for Delany,

He will win on the strand, sunny or rainy.

Now, Patrick McCullen, weaver, lived in Beabeg,

"But please, Auntie Mary, what's wrong with your leg…?"

I slipped one wet day and fell in the rain,

The broken right hip never came right again.

Now, Hanrahan's Tinkers lived at the crossroads,

"But why, Auntie Mary, do you give them loads…?"

Hush child, I'm just giving some little aid,

The children are hungry, I need some tins made.

Now Ninch was a fine place when Grimes was alive,

"Oh! Auntie Mary, see the taxi arrive…"

Well, bless my soul, indeed what you say is true,

I almost forgot, I am off to Kilnew.

"But please, Auntie Mary, tell us family links

Before you go off in the big Hillman Minx

Despite all you've said, we need to know more,

How did all these Ancestors get to Beamore?"

P.S. Who else but M.F.McC. could work out the exact relationship with the Carrolls of Dunleer, of "Death House Reilly", Father Conlon the Parish Priest, and Jimmy O'Dea the famous comedian?

Chapter Thirteen
The Legacy

The letters, which had been so much a part of Annie's life, continued to come, and record her effect on people in all parts of the country and also from abroad. Mary kept all of these as well, and a bundle of about fifty cards, telegrams and letters survives. For those who study the medical aspects of genealogy, the correspondence about her condition will be valuable. It was written to Dr. Paddy by the surgeon, Denis Farnan.

> *27, Merrion Sq.,*
> *Dublin.*
> *June 21st, 1915.*

Dear McCullen,

> *I need hardly say how I regret the termination of our case. It really illustrates what I said to you some weeks ago – that active interference, no matter how slight, seems to precipitate a virulent toxaemia, which is nearly always fatal. Still, looking back, and taking everything into consideration, I can't see that any other course was open to us; we might possibly have done the colostomy earlier, but in view of the enormous size of the growth, and its wide extension, the result must of necessity have been the same.*

> *During the short time which I knew her I developed a great regard for your poor Mother, and felt deeply the inability to help her. She was always gentle and her plaintive and questioning expression seemed to indicate that she realised all too well what was our opinion although we did not give expression to it.*

> *Very sincerely yours,*
> *Denis Farnan.*

Another view from an outside source is given in a letter of condolence from Sr. M. Raphael in the Convent of Mercy, Trim –

Since Fr. Richard's visit to us in April, when he said that his Mother was ailing, I had a strong feeling about her, and frequently gave her all of my prayers.

Likewise, the P.P. in Balbriggan writes –

The Presbytery,

Balbriggan.

June 23rd, 1915.

Dear Mr. McCullen,

...considering your dear wife's hopeless illness, it was a special mercy the good soul was spared a protracted and painful period of anxiety and trial. R.I.P...

Revd. E.D. Byrne.

Sr. Francis Reilly, writing from the Working Boys' Home at 12, Wright St., Hull –

My dear Pat,

I must let you have a little line all to yourself to convey my deepest sympathy, on the loss of your darling Annie...

What tender sympathy our poor Father would show, Pat, if he were alive, he was so fond of Pat and Annie...

Yours affectionately,

Sr. Francis Reilly.

It is often surprising how history tends to repeat itself. When I went to Oldcastle in 1964 to work as the local Agricultural Advisor, I was warned by the locals about the Hotel Owner in the Naper Arms, who they said would be "hard to deal with". I presented my credentials and said that I required to stay in the hotel – full board and meals for five days of the week. At the time, ten pounds per week would have been reasonable. He asked –

"How much do you expect to pay?"

"Well," I said, "in my last place (a shared flat in Rathmines) I paid £5, ten shillings per week." (And fed myself.)

"All right," said Mr. Andrew Carolan, "We'll settle on that ."

One of the letters from 1915 to my grandfather is from the same establishment, which must have been his haunt, on the regular visits to the fair of Oldcastle.

Naper Arms Hotel,
Oldcastle.
June 28th, 1915.

My dear Mr. McCullen,

I cannot tell you how extremely sorry both Mr. C. and myself are, for your very, very, sad bereavement in the death of Mrs. McCullen. May her soul rest in peace eternal…

Yours very sincerely,
John & K.Y. Carolan.

Referring back to the chapter on the "Lives of Reilly", there is a letter which throws more light on the relationship between Annie and Edward Reilly, the young, up and coming lawyer in America.

Schooleys Mountains,
German Valley,
New Jersey.
July 1915.

My dearest Mary,

Today's mail brought me the very, very, sad news of your dearly loved Mother's death. May God comfort you all and help you to bear your great cross – you have our greatest sympathy…The night before last, I dreamt of your dear Mother and you in B. Cunningham's, little knowing the sad news morning would bring from your Aunt May, poor dear, who feels terribly for you all.

We had a very anxious time, my brother John has had a wonderful recovery from Appendicitis. Mary Jane went to ask one of the Fathers to offer Mass for him, and he said "Sit down and talk to me, what part of the Old Country are you from? I only knew one from that part of the country, and he was a class-fellow of mine in Maynooth. His name was Dick McCullen."

What a comfort he must be to you all. <u>You should hear Edward's little ones, praying for their Papa's Godmother,</u> who we all hope is happy in Heaven, not to have any more pain or suffering.

M. Jane, Edward and John unite with me in loving sympathy to you all.

Yours affectionately,
Lissie Reilly.

After a Requiem Mass in St. Mary's Church, Annie was buried in the Family Plot at Kilsharvan. Pat had lost the love of his life, and mourned greatly. Hal was buried at Kilsharvan, beside his mother, in March of 1916.

Father Richard was appointed Diocesan Catechist, in Summer 1915, to replace Fr. Robert Kelly, and travelled by motor bike from parish to parish.

A Family Effect

The first one of Annie's children to get married was Joe, who, you may recall, was a source of "some disappointment" to Sister Anthony of Padua, as far as his academic career was concerned. One of the qualities which had been nurtured in Beamore was independence and Joe certainly had plenty of it. "The Boss" was still in mourning for Annie and Hal, but the wedding of Joe and his bride, Margaret (Sissy) Gillic, from Church Street, Oldcastle, went ahead in September of 1916, with Father Richard as the Celebrant of the Mass, John as the Best Man and May Gillic as the Bridesmaid. Sissy had been to a finishing school in Belgium and came from a home in a public house / general store, which was very akin to that of Moore's of Duleek Gate.

We can only assume that Annie would have loved every detail of the event. However, "the Boss" was in mourning, and did not attend. The photograph of the Wedding Party is a splendid one, and shows seven of Annie's children on a rare occasion, all gathered together in one place. There is an added historical dimension to the picture, in the notice hanging on the wall beside James at the back, advertising the performance of "Deirdre" in the Abbey Theatre.

Wedding Party, September 1916

Front Row (L. to R.) Mrs. Bridget Gillic, John, Joe, Sissy, May Gillic, aunt Mary Jane Macken, Tom Gillic.

Middle Row (L. to R.) ___?, Fr. Robert Barry P.P., Oldcastle, Fr. Denis Flynn P.P., St. Mary's, Fr. Richard, Mary F., Dr. Paddy, Kate McCullen Lynch, Anthony.

Back Row (L. to R.) Patrick Macken, Henry McCullen, Fr. Michael Farrelly, James.

It is an interesting statistic that when Annie died in June of 1915 at the age of 60 years, she had no grandchild. In 2003, there are 146 descendents spread over four continents. The possibility of a photograph of all these would be remote, but when a "Family Gathering" was organized in Beamore in 1994, we managed to get 120, including some in-laws, in a field at the old Beaubec monastic site, for a Mass celebrated by Fr. Richard McCullen C.M., nephew of Father Richard.

"Family Gathering", 1994

Enduring Qualities

Reflecting on all of the letters and other memorabilia and on Annie's hectic sixty years, the qualities which surface again and again can be listed as follows –

- ❖ Independence
- ❖ Empathy
- ❖ Humour and Wit
- ❖ Storytelling
- ❖ Management Ability
- ❖ Spirituality and Love

The continuing effect of such traits has been brought home to me on many occasions, even at a remove of nearly a century. This is well-illustrated by my experience when applying for a position as Temporary Instructor in Agriculture in County Meath in 1964. The bestowing of such a posting lay in the hands of the twenty members of the County Committee of Agriculture, who were a mixture of political appointees and elected councilors. All other things being equal, natives of Meath got preference, but the candidate just had to get to get up on their scooter and visit all the power brokers and members to canvass a vote. The jobs were eagerly sought after, so there was always a long list of aspirants.

I procured a list of the twenty members, and sallied forth. On the way through Kells, I called to the parochial house, to consult Uncle Dick. When I explained my purpose, he smiled and said, "I won't canvass anyone, whatever needs to be done is done already. You will be o.k." He was almost eighty at the time and I wondered at his confidence. I called to see Joe's son, Thos, at Clonmellon, and we visited some of the important people. After two weeks of criss-crossing the county, I had seen all the twenty. The day of the vote came, and I received fourteen votes, with the next candidate on nine. I met him afterwards and he said, "I knew I could not beat you, my uncle is only a Parish Priest, yours is a Monsignor."

The care and devotion shown to their different flocks, by Fr. Richard and Dr. Paddy, has continued to reverberate down the years and surfaces in the most unusual places. In 1984, I had an important meeting about Gas Grid extension, at the Shelbourne Hotel in Dublin. Arriving with no minutes to spare, I drove into the hotel car park, without any kind of document to prove my entitlement to anything. It was full, and the attendant said,

"No hope, Sir, there are several waiting."

"Oh gosh, I have an important meeting in the hotel – my name is McCullen…"

"Did you say McCullen?"

"Yes."

"Would you be anything to Dr. McCullen?"

"He is my Godfather."

"Well, what do you know? He saved my life…the ould throat, he did a marvelous job…here give me your keys and I'll sort something out."

At that time, Dr. Paddy was dead for thirty-two years, but his son, Oliver, was practicing as an ear, nose and throat surgeon.

All of Annie's offspring were of an independent nature. When researching for the parish history book in 1984, I called to see Jemmy Dyas, in Duleek Street, who was then an old blind man. He was most welcoming, although the Dyases were a docker family and known as tough people. Jemmy explained his welcome. When his father died in July 1918, the mother was left with a large family, as a young widow. Some of the lads had work in the docks, on a casual basis, and the work was vital to family finances. Funerals were fixed for two o'clock but this did not fit with the dock schedule and Fr. Flynn refused to change the funeral time. Mrs. Mary Ann Dyas was distraught, so she went to Pat McCullen to see what she could do. He sent for Fr. Richard, who agreed to deal with the funeral ceremonies at six in the evening when the dock work was finished. The young Catechist duly arrived on the motor bike, dealt with the burial of James Dyas, and Father Flynn was not too pleased. In 1984, I got the credit from Jemmy – "I'll never forget it to you, young McCullen…your Aunt Mary prepared me for my First Communion and I loved all the McCullens in Beamore…and Captain, oh, he was the best horse ever pulled a cart, I loved him too!" He sat at the kitchen table in Corporation Cottages, and the tears ran down his cheeks. Even though the motor bike had long since ceased its irregular put-put-put, the kind deed of the rider still rattled on. My poem of 1999 tries to capture the benefits of carrying a worthy name or face into the 21st Century.

The Family Face

"Come in, and be welcome," the Old Woman said
Your Uncle, the Monsignor, buried our dead.
The Lady of the pub said, "Pour him a drink!
The Carpenter's Guild has been our common link."

"I will sell you the field," spoke a weary voice,
"Your Grandfather gave us the house of our choice."
"Park your car safe, in here beside the Shelbourne,
Your Godfather did me a lifelong good turn."

"As long as you wish, you can have B & B
For the man from Meath was a good friend to me."
"You are sure of a vote from Fianna Fáil,
Joe and Thos helped me when business was small."

"I will not charge a bill for leaving it right,
Your Uncle, the Doctor, came often by night."
"I will polish the table, straighten the legs,
Mrs. Mac was a lady who gave me duck eggs."

"The Board has made it's firm and final offers –
Brother of Pat's? Well, I'll look in the coffers."
"We do not send reporters, as normal rule…
Who did you say? A brother of McCool?"

"Do some research?" said the Trinity man,
"Related to Dermot? I'm sure we can."
There is no other ghost I can embrace
But enjoy the haunting of the Family Face.

Writing in the "Meath Chronicle" in 1977, in an obituary on "Monsignor McCullen", Garret Fox describes him as "a noted educationalist, Greek scholar, protector of orphans, most helpful Confessor, doer of good deeds by stealth, doyen of the clergy of the Meath Diocese and only honorary citizen of Kells." He dressed in a woolen blanket to keep warm, refused all gifts of a material kind and requested the plainest of wooden coffins for himself. The Kells Urban District Council eventually decided on a mutually acceptable form of recognition, by naming a 36-house development on the Virginia road, as "Father McCullen Park". When Doctor Paddy died quite suddenly at the age of 64 years in 1952, the writer of the obituary in the "Drogheda Independent" said of him – "To his patients he was something more than a doctor, for indeed, it can be said that he was their guide, philosopher and very sincere friend; a man who gave all and sought little in return, but earthly glory or fame were not his desire."

Empathy

When Annie awaited the postman and her letters in Kilkee, she used the phrase, "I felt like a little girl." This ability to walk in the shoes of a child or any other person, was an outstanding trait of hers and it also moved into succeeding generations. The letter of Fr. Richard to his nephew Oliver is a classic example. It is written from the President of St. Finian's College, to a nine-year old boy.

St. Finian's College,
April 4ᵗʰ, 1933.

My dear Oliver,

Yes: the way the whistle is made in "Our Boys" is almost the same as the way old Pat Fay showed me forty years ago. But I think that the sap would have to be running freely up and down from the roots to the leaves along the skin, and that happens only in summer. In winter and early spring, the skin is quite dry and hard and it is impossible to shift it from the wood inside without breaking it. I'll try if boiling it or soaking it in hot water or steam will be of any use. If not, we shall have to wait for the soft ash shoots or sallies in the summer time.

Regards to you and Dick,
R. MacCullen.

Oliver McCullen, aged 9

Humour

Referring back to the letters of James to his Mother while he laboured, under duress, in the Seminary in Navan, you may recall his dry humour and wit. It appears that this was picked up from Annie. Many years later, in 1923, at the mature age of 42 years, he married Annie Grimes from Skerries, who was a spirited, good-looking lady. He was a big man with a heavy moustache, a tendency to rotundness, corduroy trousers and a check sports coat, and a head of hair that did not respond to brush or comb. Annie was graceful and ladylike, with a developed dress sense and a very determined chin. The combination of that chin, and James' unmanageable hair led to a creative tension which was not hidden from anyone who came in contact with them.

She spent the next generation trying – in vain – to mould her James into something more of a gentleman. They had three daughters, and the more female the household became, the more he felt that he had to redress the balance with male behaviour. James wore a heavy frieze coat at jobs around the farm, and the garment developed a pronounced aroma of "animal" about it. In modern terms, it smelled of brute. For many years, she had tried to wash the coat, given him gifts of new coats, and suggested that it was gone beyond even his standards of acceptability. In all efforts, she failed. Eventually driven to desperation, she waited until James went to a fair for two days, and stole the overcoat.

Determined to end the matter for once and for all, she dug a hole in the field outside the house and buried the garment. This seemed like the perfect crime, and when James returned and remarked that his "good coat" was missing, she feigned innocence. A week passed and the plan seemed to be a success, until Mary Frances arrived from Beamore on a visit. Innocently, Annie mentioned her triumph but forgot that blood is thicker than water or sisterly solidarity. Mary took pity on James' searching in vain and dropped a few hints.

He said nothing, slipped away with the spade, and appeared for dinner, dressed in the subterranean coat, complete with various inhabitants of the soil, and a new aroma, caused by mixing "brute" with "mud pack".

Storytelling

The public lives, and service to their communities, of Fr. Richard and Dr. Paddy are more easily found, than those of the other children of Annie Moore-McCullen, John, Joe and Anthony. All these three shared a love of storytelling with the older four, and could visit each other and swop stories endlessly, and the more outrageous the yarn, the better. In his retirement, Joe lived at St. Margaret's, in Laytown, and my job was to keep him in firewood, seasoned and ready to burn. The fact that I had worked for five years from Lough Sheelin to Diamor, and all around Oldcastle meant that the nuances of his stories were appreciated. He would tell of a roadside dweller, a young man from Moylagh, who was planting cabbage plants in the garden, when he spied a recruiting sergeant and party approaching, on the lookout for young able men, for service in the British Army. They had seen him at a distance, and he knew his fate was inevitable. As he watched, and feared conscription, he thought of a good ploy. He started to plant the cabbages upside down, with the leaves buried, and the roots sticking up in the air. When they drew alongside he laughed and skipped and asked the officer to inspect his garden. One glance was enough for the sergeant to realize that the young man was mentally retarded, and the raiding party kept moving on in search of stable, alert types more suitable for trench warfare, while our friend celebrated his escape.

My father's stories usually revolved around confrontations on matters of principle with some villain or other. He had a unique ability to dress down offenders and give them a lecture on the rights of Man, and still end up making a friend for life, whether it was with the Civic Guard who was stealing his tree for firewood during the Emergency, the Teacher who was mistreating his boys, or the Itinerant who put in horses overnight to eat his grass and removed them before daylight came.

Mr. Neeson was such a traveling man, and he used to put his horses in at ten o'clock and remove them at six in the morning. John sallied forth with his small sons, myself included, early one morning, and rustled the horses to lock them up in a yard at Beamore. A day later, Mr. Neeson came to ask for the animals to be returned and offered restitution. It was insufficient, even though Mr. Neeson offered a cheque to be written by his ten-year old son, and the case ended up in the District Court, where John won the case, and was awarded six pence, as token damages. Himself and Neeson discovered they both knew a local Doctor, Gerald Costello, who was a native of Co. Fermanagh, and on this basis, peace was declared, and midnight grazing ceased.

We can only conclude that Annie enjoyed the adventures of her children, and encouraged them to regale the family with stories from outside the farm gate. Anthony specialized in mimicry and the strange doings of the people who lived around Pluckamin, Clonalvey and Ardcath, near to the border of Fingal. When he would arrive, for a visit to Beamore, we were sitting and ready for the latest instalment of adventure in the lives of Meehawl, Crawley or the Johnson brothers, all of whom seemed to lead an existence of excitement far beyond our experiences. The drama was delivered as a one-man-show, and Anthony would play all the parts and the different voices himself, and we loved it.

Good Management

All of Annie's immediate family had these traits in common, and yet were all utterly different characters. Her larger group of descendents await some scientific examination to see how they have related to her. The ability to manage their affairs, both in domestic and business matters, was evident in Mary and her brothers and a very good example of this is the building and completion of so many schools in Kells and especially of the new St. Columcille's Church, which was opened in October 1960 at a cost of £120,000 and all of this was paid for before the opening. His memories of the hardship of Seminary life helped to motivate many improvements to the living conditions at St. Finian's in Mullingar, during his Presidency of the College from 1921-1933, and he also provided a spacious gym for the establishment. There is little doubt that access to management decisions and the power to control their own affairs, at an early stage in life, makes for good managers, and this freedom to take on big tasks seems likely to have had its' origins in Annie's style of mothering.

Spirituality and Love

Along with the wedding apparel and plaits of hair, another item discovered in the secure safe in the farmhouse was the prayer book of Annie, well-thumbed and used, the small book, five inches by four, nevertheless contains over 800 pages and includes Masses, various devotions and prayers and a Rule of Life section, plus Catechism and Biblical readings. Regular prayer seems to have been an integral part of her life, not just during the time of illness, but from her schooldays, and membership of the Children of Mary, with Lizzie Donor. There is no evidence of hypocritical piety, but a strong common-sensed faith and Christianity, in both Annie and Pat, and their offspring.

The various debates of the period 1870-1915, where the views of the Papacy, the Irish Bishops and different groups of clergy and classes of Society, were seen to differ over land reform, Parnell's leadership, shades of Nationalism from ultra constitutional to physical force, and recruiting campaigns for the British Army, are reflected in a healthy independence shown in Annie's correspondence. On some issues, Father Curry might be right, and on others, not so right. What is clear enough from the well-used state of the Family Bible and Butler's "Lives of the Saints", each in two volumes, is that spiritual reading was a daily practice.

My father told me that "the Boss" always read a page of the "Lives of the Saints" each night, when he was at home. This meant that one saint was covered per day, and when we look up Saint Anne, she is extolled as the one who deserves special veneration, as a patroness of education and marriage. Annie Moore certainly lived up to these ideals, and Pat realised what a splendid, unique lady his wife had been. In 1924, he took his store of gold sovereigns to a goldsmith and requested that they be melted down and cast into a gold chalice to give to Father Richard. The goldsmith explained that such melting was illegal but that he would of course be glad to craft a chalice, to the value of the store of sovereigns. This was agreed, and the inscription, in Latin, translates "Patrick McCullen, mindful of the goodness of God, give this chalice to my son Richard, 1924."

After considering over three hundred letters and a span of forty-eight years, the only conclusion I can come to is that Annie Moore was a charming, beautiful, funny, accomplished and loving woman, and a granny that the 146 have had every reason to be proud of. It is fitting that the last words should be those of three of her great correspondents.

Lizzie

"I know your heart is too good and too noble." August 21st, 1870

Mary Monica

"I really do not know how to thank you for your kindness." December 23rd, 1877

Sister Anthony of Padua

"If I do any good in this life, it is to Annie, I owe it; a more devoted daughter, sister, wife and mother could not be." June 21st, 1915

Drogheda Argus, June 26th, 1915
Obituary
Death of Mrs. Patrick McCullen, Beamore.

Announcement received with deep regret on Monday…a devout and fervent member of the Catholic Church…an ideal mother and a sincere friend, her death will cause a void in the family circle which will never be filled…Her generosity to the Church and to the poor was well known, and while the former has lost an earnest and practical daughter, who gave generously of her family to its' mission, the latter have lost a friend in need…The funeral was of remarkably large dimensions and of all denominations, while all the business houses on the route were shuttered…it would be impossible to give anything like a full list of those present…

Appendix

John Sheil the Poet, who lived from the 1780s to 1872 and spent a considerable part of his long life in Drogheda, wrote many songs about local people and events. Two of these would have been sung in Annie's own time and the third was the party piece of the McCullens of Beabeg, at wedding feasts and other celebrations. It was written by John Broderick, who was not invited to that particular wedding in Baltray. John Sheil is buried in the Cord Cemetery, Drogheda.

Sweet Dooley Gate

Sweet Dooley Gate, sweet Dooley Gate, it's the place I do adore,
Where all young men and maidens they dwelt in it before;
Where all young men and maidens they now lie far away,
They are not in sweet Dooley Gate, but they're in Americay.

My young love's name I'll not exclaim, he's proper, tall and straight,
He is the finest young man that walks round Dooley Gate,
He is the finest young man of any I did see,
And in spite of all our enemies I'll keep his company.

There's some speaks ill of my true love and there's more speaks ill of me,
But let them all say what they will I'll keep his company,
And let them all say what they will, I'll do the best I can,
And it's soon I'll be leaving St. Mary's Mills for to marry that young man.

'Twould break my heart if I had to part from the lad that I do adore,
He said that he would marry me and we'd leave old Erin's shore;
He named the day, the month of May, he did not hesitate,
And it's soon we'll be leaving old Drogheda and dear old Dooley Gate.

Sweet Dooley Gate, sweet Dooley Gate, it's the place I do adore,

Where all young men and maidens they dwelt in it before;

Where all young men and maidens they now lie far away,

They are not in sweet Dooley Gate, but they're in Americay.

The Flower of Beamore

Attend all you young men that have felt Cupid's dart!

Draw near and you'll hear what has caused me to smart:

In pain I'll remain, my tender heart sore

For Nancy, my fancy, the Flower of Beamore!

She is neat and complete, this fair maid that I love,

Devine and benign and as mild as a dove.

She is sweet and discreet and till death I'll adore

Young Nancy, my fancy, the Flower of Beamore.

No creature in nature with her can compare

For manner and honour and wit, I declare

She's the rarest and fairest on Erin's green shore,

That's Nancy, my fancy, the Flower of Beamore.

Aurora or Flora my love can't surpass,

Diana, Susannah or Paris's lass,

Her smile would beguile Alexander of yore,

That's Nancy, my fancy, the Flower of Beamore.

By Cupid, I'm stupid and sorely oppressed,

Annoyed and destroyed and bereft of all rest.

I am torn and forlorn and I'm tortured all o'er

With Nancy, my fancy, the Flower of Beamore.

I'm inclined to decline and to lay down my pen

Because she will not love me, I'm the outcast of men.

Until death stops my breath, the sad loss I'll deplore

Of Nancy, my fancy, the Flower of Beamore.

The Wedding of Sweet Baltray

'Twas in the pleasant Summertime I roved along the river Boyne,

To take the air I was inclined, Dame Nature seemed so gay,

And as I walked I chanced to meet a friend sincere who did me greet,

And straight 'way asked me most discreet to come to sweet Baltray.

I then complied with his demand — he gave me sure to understand,

His uncle's son would give his hand upon that very day,

And in wedlock band he would be tied unto a brisk and virtuous bride,

And it's at the fun he would provide that night in sweet Baltray.

For to pull foot we did agree and paced the road being full of glee,

This pleasant pastime for to see without the least delay,

And at length we reached this wishful place where nuptial joys they filled each face,

We welcomed were to mirth and feast that night in sweet Baltray.

Young Lark-Heeled Dick with Nosey Kate attended at the marriage trate,

And Mangey Ned with his bald pate came there with Nell McKay,

And Blared-Eyed Bob and Blind Moll Brown and Teague McShane for Mornington,

That made the jovial toast go round that night in Sweet Baltray.

Now the groom was called Ould Sluggin' Jack — he had a horrid humpy back,

His teeth were rotten, blue and black, his eyes were shining grey,

And to crown the joke his nose was big, likewise he wore a frizzed-up wig,

He snored and grunted like a pig that night in sweet Baltray.

The bride was aged about sixty-three — she had one leg off above the knee —

Without a guide she couldn't see to walk the King's highway,

And besides she had a monstrous scab with the mild itch that's twice as bad,

Her equal sure could not be had that night in sweet Baltray.

To close the matrimonial knot this charming pair it's up they got,

The words they said upon the spot at which all cried "Hurray!"

Then the people wished them all good joy, and every year a darling boy,

The bride she winked and did reply, "Success to sweet Baltray!"

Good Irish whiskey was produced at which McShane he did play loose,

Said Blared-Eyed Bob, "I love the juice of barley every day."

Says Mangey Ned to Lark-Heeled Dick, "I'm sure we both will love this trick —

We'll drink all night suppose we're sick and ne'er can leave Baltray."

The bride and groom they did suggest that they would really do their best,

So up they got upon the chest a few steps to display,

So Mangey Ned tuned up his trump and Sluggin' Jack he shook his stump,

Lame Nan beat time with her odd stump that night in sweet Baltray.

"Moll Roe" it was the only tune this couple jigged about the room,

Jack loaded like a bee in June and Nan said, "Leave me way,

For when I get straight upon me prop I'll tip the loft with every hop,

For neighbours dear, I'm in me shop this night in sweet Baltray!"

I stood then round just for to view this comic, jovial, hearty crew,

For in all my life I never knew a company so gay,

For some told stories, some sang songs and more they danced and waltzed along,

The bagpipes sounded clear and strong that night in sweet Baltray.

With tranquil pleasure and delight and matchless fun we spent the night,

We clapped and cheered with all out might 'till near the break of day,

So Jack and Nan away were led and instantly were put to bed,

We all shook hands and away we fled away from sweet Baltray.